DISTINCTIVE LESSONS
FROM LUKE

William C. Brownson, Jr.

Contemporary Discussion Series

BAKER BOOK HOUSE
Grand Rapids, Michigan

TO HELEN
My greatest encourager in applying
the truth of the gospel

ISBN: 0-8010-0626-0

Printed in the United States of America

CONTENTS

1

DID IT REALLY HAPPEN?

*Inasmuch as many have undertaken to compile
a narrative of the things which have been accomplished among us, just as they were deliv-
ered to us by those who from the beginning
were eyewitnesses and ministers of the word, it
seemed good to me also, having followed all
things closely for some time past, to write an
orderly account for you, most excellent Theophilus, that you may know the truth concerning
the things of which you have been informed
(Luke 1:1-4).*

Many of us are fairly well informed about the
Christian faith. We have been exposed to Christian
preaching; we have shared to some degree in the life
of a congregation; and we know at least in broad outline what the Bible has to say. Most of us have also
known Christian people in whom we have seen the
faith in action. Some, it may be, have been forced to
meet sophisticated challenges to the Christian faith,
while others have known a more sheltered experience
in which their convictions were seldom called into
question. But there are very few of us in the seventies
who have not grappled in some way with questions
about the historical basis of what we've been taught.
Did it really happen—happen in the way we've been
told?

The Gospel according to Luke is designed to deal
with precisely that issue. Luke, the only one of the
Gospel writers who addressed his work to an individ-

ual, wrote to a man of some rank and distinction in the Roman empire with this announced purpose: "That you may know the truth concerning the things of which you have been informed" (1:4). Luke assumes that Theophilus has heard about the faith, perhaps from a number of different sources. He wants to assure him that these things are worthy of belief. He wants to confirm him in the confidence that the Christian message is historically true.

Luke makes clear at the outset his concern with the facts of the case. His announced focus is "the things which have been accomplished among us" or, as the NEB renders it, "the events that have happened among us" (1:1). To this Gospel writer, in other words, Christianity centers not in abstract doctrines or in moral precepts but rather in *happenings*. More than any other evangelist, Luke is at great pains to place the Gospel story in a definite historical setting.

He, for example, is the only one who refers to the decree of Caesar Augustus that there should be a general census (2:1). He alone makes specific mention that this enrollment took place "when Quirinius was governor of Syria" (2:2). And when Luke comes to record the beginning of John the Baptist's ministry, he goes into considerable detail to tell his readers that this was during the fifteenth year of the reign of Tiberius Caesar, and to show who were the leading political and religious personalities of this time (3:1-2). Luke has no myths or fables to relate. Nor is he merely conveying timeless truths. Rather, he is telling how and in precisely what circumstances certain things happened.

In his concern to "tell it like it was," Luke went

to the most reliable sources for his information. What he has to say comes directly from "those who from the beginning were eyewitnesses and ministers of the Word" (1:2). Luke was not one of the original twelve apostles, nor does he claim to be himself an eyewitness of the things he relates. But we know that he was closely associated with the apostle Paul and with other leaders in the first-century church. Like every good historian, he went to the primary sources. Moreover, this information was not difficult to secure. At the time Luke wrote, many others had already written narratives of these things, based upon the same eyewitness reports. Luke seems to imply that at least in broad outline these things had become widely known. In fact, he quotes Paul as saying of King Agrippa, "I am persuaded that none of these things has escaped his notice, for this was not done in a corner" (Acts 26:26).

But while acknowledging that a number of others have compiled narratives of these things, Luke makes a rather special claim for his own work. It, too, deals with things that have happened and with the reports of eyewitnesses, but Luke seems to have done research beyond that of any of his predecessors. He has "followed all things closely for some time past" (1:3). Further, he has sought to produce an orderly account. His is not simply a random collection of certain works and sayings of Jesus. It seeks to deal in a comprehensive way with the foundations of the Christian message.

But, someone objects, even though Luke claims to have consulted these eyewitnesses and to have done all this research, how do we know that he really is a reliable historian? Good question. There were New

Testament scholars during the last century who regarded Luke's writings as hopelessly unreliable. More recently, however, researches conducted by a number of outstanding scholars have brought information to light which confirms again and again Luke's historical accuracy. Sir William Ramsay, who began his extensive studies throughout Asia Minor with great suspicions about this historical data, was led to say at the conclusion of his work that "Luke's history is unsurpassed in respect to its trustworthiness." Professor Otto Piper could make this sweeping statement: "Wherever modern scholarship has been able to check up on the accuracy of Luke's work, the judgment has been unanimous: He is one of the finest and ablest historians in the ancient world."

"But how can we be sure that this is what Luke actually wrote?" asks someone else. Aren't even the earliest New Testament manuscripts separated from the time of Luke's writing by hundreds of years? Again, this is a very legitimate inquiry. Let's approach it by comparing Luke with other ancient historians. Tacitus, for example, who wrote early in the second century about events half a century earlier, is considered a reliable source for the period in spite of the fact that the oldest manuscript copy of his work dates from a thousand years after he wrote. There is a similar thousand-year period between the writing of Caesar's *Gallic Wars* and the date of the oldest extant manuscripts. Yet these manuscripts are considered excellent historical sources. The evidence for the Gospel according to Luke and the rest of the New Testament is incomparably superior. Over four thousand Greek manuscripts are still in existence. And some of the best date from 300 or 400 years after the composition of the Gospels. We have smaller portions that can be reliably dated in the first half of the second century.

Now it can be argued that we cannot be absolutely certain about anything that happened in ancient history. And that position cannot be "disproved." There is no way to prove anything that happened in the past if by proof we mean mathematical or laboratory demonstration. But if we believe that the study of history makes any sense at all, we must acknowledge that the evidence for what Luke has recorded about Jesus Christ is far more impressive and reliable than that regarding any other person in ancient history.

Does this prove then that Christianity rests upon a divine revelation and that Luke's Gospel is inspired by God? No, it doesn't. But it does lend strong support for those convictions. The Holy Spirit must create faith in a human heart, but in doing so he makes use of evidence. Believing that Luke is historically reliable will not, of course, make a person a Christian. True faith involves a personal trust in, and commitment to, the Christ revealed in this Gospel. But what Luke's writing does provide is the assurance that the person who makes such a commitment is not taking a leap into the dark. Because of what Luke and others have written, Theophilus and millions like him can "know the truth concerning the things of which they have been informed." Those who have committed themselves to Christ may exult with deep confidence that the Gospel story is "for real." God made it happen—just that way.

1. *Why does Luke place such great emphasis on historical events? What does this suggest about the nature of Chrisitanity as compared with other religions?*
2. *What steps must we follow to gain reliable information about the life and teachings of* any *person who lived long ago?*
3. *Does Luke's use of various written sources raise problems with regard to our belief in the inspiration of the Scriptures? How?*
4. *How would you present the Christian message to a person who does not believe that the Bible is divinely inspired?*
5. *Is believing that certain events took place (Christ's life, miracles, death, resurrection) the same as believing in Christ? If not, what is the difference?*
6. *What has made faith "come alive" for you?*

2

THE OLD AND THE NEW

Background Scripture—Luke 1:5-24

But the angel said to him, "Do not be afraid, Zechariah, for your prayer is heard, and your wife Elizabeth will bear you a son, and you shall call his name John. And you will have joy and gladness, and many will rejoice at his birth; for he will be great before the Lord, and he shall drink no wine nor strong drink, and he will be filled with the Holy Spirit, even from his mother's womb. And he will turn many of the sons of Israel to the Lord their God, and he will go before him in the spirit and power of Elijah, to turn the heart of the fathers to the children, and the disobedient to the wisdom of the just, to make ready for the Lord a people prepared" (Luke 1:13-17).

Matthew, Mark, and John tell us nothing about the conception and birth of John the Baptist. Luke, however, relates these circumstances in great detail and sets them at the very beginning of his Gospel. Why this special interest in John?

We have already seen that Luke is keenly interested in history. He wants his readers to know the historical circumstances in which the great events of the Gospel have occurred. But Luke's great interest is not in history as such, but in history as the setting, the arena in which God's saving purpose is accomplished. Accordingly, he seeks at the outset to show how the good news of Jesus Christ is related to God's past acts in the calling and career of Israel.

Luke sees the appearance of John the Baptist as the culmination of Israel's history.

Notice how the narrative gives expression to this. John, it is emphasized, comes from a priestly family. His father was a priest of the division of Abijah; his mother, Elizabeth, was of priestly descent. To be both a priest and the husband of a priest's daughter was considered a mark of double honor. And concerning a woman of fine character it was often said, "She deserves to be married to a priest." John springs from this Levitical line—from the family in Israel which was especially set apart to the service of God.

It is noted also that Zechariah and Elizabeth "were both righteous before God, walking in all the commandments and ordinances of the Lord blameless" (v. 6). They were upright in character, seeking to live all of life as under God's eye, and therefore were fitted to represent the highest form of Old Testament piety. John came, in other words, from that remnant within Israel which was truly faithful to God.

Further, the announcement of his birth was made by the angel to Zechariah is the holy place of the temple. The temple was the center of Israel's faith and life, the chief token of God's presence in her midst. And since the word of God's promise is always a creative word, bringing to pass the very thing which it announces, there is a sense in which John's appearance actually originates with the temple. Finally, the announcement comes at the most hallowed moment of Jewish worship. The privilege of offering the incense fell to the lot of a priest only once in his lifetime. As the incense was offered, symbolic of true consecration to God, and as the people gathered for prayer in the outer temple court, the heavenly message came that John was to be born. His birth is thus connected with the summit of Jewish worship. It comes as God's answer to the age-old prayers and longings of his people.

Even the names of the persons involved are significant. The young child is to be named John, which in Hebrew means "the Lord is merciful" or "the gracious gift of God." The name of his father Zechariah, means "the Lord remembers," and Elizabeth can be translated "my God is an oath" or "my God is the faithful one." In the names of this little family, then, are pledged the faithfulness of God to his covenant, and the gift of his grace. Everything points to the fact that the saving Lord who has been active in Israel's history is at work now in some supreme way on behalf of his people.

What is prophesied about John's future career fits in perfectly with this theme. His birth will bring great rejoicing. He will follow in the exalted Nazirite tradition, drinking neither wine nor strong drink. Whereas the Holy Spirit during Old Testament days came upon God's servants from time to time to fit them for special tasks, John will know the sustained influences of the Spirit. He will be filled with the Holy Spirit even from his mother's womb. His work, we learn, will be the work of a prophet. Like a true spokesman for God he will call many back to the ways of the Lord. He will be the special prophet of whom Malachi spoke, ministering in the spirit and the power of the great Elijah. He will fulfill the best in the noble tradition of Israelite prophecy.

Now put the pieces of the picture together. John's birth, as Luke describes it, takes place in a setting of worship, crowning both the priestly and prophetic traditions, and bringing a joyous fulfillment of God's ancient covenant. Does this seem to accord to John's birth almost too high a place? Really, what more could be said even about the birth of the Messiah? But in all this, Luke clearly keeps John in the role of a prophet, a forerunner. He is not the Lord but he will "go before" the Lord. His advent is not an end in itself, but "to make ready for the Lord a people prepared" (v. 17).

Here Luke is in accord with the rest of the Gospel tradition. When he compares John with all that has preceded, he gives him a supreme place: "I tell you, among those born of women, none is greater than John" (7:28). In the eyes of Christ, he is a prophet "and more than a prophet" (7:26). But when compared with the advent of Jesus and the dawning new age, John is distinctly subordinate. He goes before the Lord to prepare his ways, but he himself confesses that one mightier than he is coming, the thong of whose sandals he is not worthy to untie. Indeed, as Jesus says, "he who is least in the kingdom of God is greater" than John (7:28).

To Luke, then, John the Baptist completes the old covenant. He is its last, best representative. He embodies in his person and ministry all that God was seeking to say to the world in the history of Israel. But in John, the old covenant is both fulfilled and transcended. In him, the whole history of God's Israel does what it was intended to do—it prepares for and points to the coming Lord. This is its true message. Now it is seen that neither priest nor prophet, neither temple nor temple worship has ultimate significance in God's plan. Even the hallowed Old Testament Scriptures find their highest meaning only as they testify to Jesus Christ. As the risen Lord was later to teach his disciples: "Everything written about me in the law of Moses and the prophets and the psalms must be fulfilled."

Luke's unique record of John's birth bears a double message. It demonstrates that in the good news of Christ there is both continuity and newness—the consummation of an old age and the dawning of a new. Luke, like his fellow evangelist John, sees in John the Baptist the summing up of the old covenant. To both writers, John is a finger pointing and a voice heralding: "Behold the Lamb of God who takes away the sin of the world."

John the Baptist, as Luke presents him, is the model for the witnessing church. He is what we ought to be. When we look at him, we see God's hand in history, but we see more than that. We see John pointing us not to the past, nor to himself, but to the living, saving, coming Lord.

1. *What is "special" about Luke's interest in history? In what sense is his Gospel like a biography? How is it different?*

2. *How is John the Baptist related to the Old Covenant? To the New Covenant?*

3. *How is John unique among the prophets? How is he subordinate to Jesus?*

4. *From the evidence given in the Gospels, how would you say that John differed from Jesus in personality and life-style?*

5. *How does John the Baptist serve as a pattern for the life and witness of God's people?*

6. *In what sense is all our Christian faith and experience a blending of "the old and the new"?*

14

THE VIRGIN MARY:
PATTERN FOR PROTESTANTS

Background Scripture—Luke 1:26-56

And the angel said to her, "The Holy Spirit will come upon you, and the power of the Most High will overshadow you; therefore the child to be born will be called holy, the Son of God. And behold, your kinswoman Elizabeth in her old age has also conceived a son; and this is the sixth month with her who was called barren. For with God nothing will be impossible." And Mary said, "Behold I am the handmaid of the Lord; let it be to me according to your word." And the angel departed from her (Luke 1:35-38).

Most Protestants find themselves perplexed and annoyed by Roman Catholic dogma about the Virgin Mary. Few of us can understand or appreciate, for example, the teaching that Mary was preserved from all stain of sin and made incapable of sinning by an "immaculate conception." The doctrine that she was "taken up body and soul into heavenly glory upon the completion of her earthly sojourn" causes similar difficulties. And who among us can feel comfortable when titles like Co-Mediatrix, Co-Redemptrix, and Queen of Heaven are assigned to Mary? We object to these dogmas and ascriptions because we find no basis for them in Scripture and, at a deeper level, because they tend to obscure the centrality and sufficiency of Jesus Christ as the one Savior.

15

What many Protestants do not realize, however, is that there are similar currents of feeling within the Roman Catholic Church itself. Although the Second Vatican Council did not revise any dogmas about the Virgin Mary or condemn the titles of veneration attributed to her, it did set forth this profoundly important principle: These titles "are to be so understood that they neither take away from nor add anything to the dignity and efficacy of Christ, the one Mediator." In this we may all rejoice.

For the most part, however, Protestants have been content with negative statements about the Virgin Mary (what is *not* true about her). In reaction against what seems an over-emphasis upon her significance for the life of the church, many of us have missed this significance entirely. Unwilling to look upon her as an object of faith, we have failed to see in her even a pattern *for* faith. Here we have lost something—and here our Roman Catholic brethren can instruct us. Vatican II calls her "the Church's model, an excellent exemplar in faith." It follows Ambrose of Milan in teaching that Mary "is a model of the Church in the matter of faith, charity, and perfect union with Christ."

We are indebted to the Gospel according to Luke for almost all we know about the Virgin Mary. Only Luke tells us of the divine announcement made to Mary, of her visit to Elizabeth, and of her songs of praise. Only he opens to us something of what was in the young mother's mind. He alone gives us a glimpse of her dealings with Jesus in the days of his youth. Were it not for Luke we would not know that Mary was with the disciples in the upper room after the ascension of our Lord, and that she shared in the Spirit's outpouring at Pentecost. And it is supremely in his writings that she appears as a woman of faith, a pattern for believers.

Think first of Mary as one who *received the gift of God's grace*. "Do not be afraid, Mary," announced the angel, "for you have found favor with God." This is a rephrasing of his earlier greeting, "Hail, O favored one, the Lord is with you." In each case the root of the words translated "favor" and "favored" is the New Testament word for "grace." Grace means the unmerited love of God toward us. Here no achievement of Mary's, no special virtue of hers is being singled out for praise. In fact, there is no mention of anything in Mary which could have been deserving of favor.

Grace means that the initiative is all with God. Mary is a pattern for believers in that before she can believe, she must receive the gift of God's grace. Isn't that precisely Paul's teaching? "For by grace ye have been saved, through faith, and this is not your own doing, it is the gift of God—not because of works, lest any man should boast" (Eph. 2:8, 9).

Further, the gift which is given to Mary is the grace granted to every believer—Jesus Christ himself. At the deepest level, grace is not a substance or an influence but a person. It is not something, but Someone—the Savior himself. By the miraculous action of the Holy Spirit the body of Jesus was formed in the womb of the Virgin Mary, and by the same miraculous action of the Holy Spirit the now risen Christ takes up his abode in every believing heart.

Mary is a model for the church also in her response to God's gift. After the staggering announcement of the angel that she would be the mother of the Son of God, Mary said, "Behold, I am the hand-maid of the Lord; let it be to me according to your word." Here is *submission to the gracious will of God*. The New Testament calls this elsewhere, "the obedience of faith."

At first glance Mary's submission may not seem very significant. An unspeakable honor and privilege was being bestowed upon her—why shouldn't she embrace such a prospect with joy and eagerness? But this is to forget some of the practical realities of her situation. For a betrothed woman to be found pregnant before her marriage could mean divorce, ostracism, and even death. Mary could only guess at what might lie ahead for her of misunderstanding and rejection. It was not a small thing for her to say, "Let it be to me according to your word."

Obedience and faith have been linked together from the very beginning in God's covenant with his people. Abraham, father of the faithful, discovered in the strange command to offer up his son, Isaac, that faith leads to a costly commitment, to following God's will even when it means losing the dearest thing in life. Mary, too, in accepting God's plan, faced the possible loss of Joseph, her betrothed. The same faith was to lead later to a still more costly sacrifice. Mary learned from Simeon that her son would be "a sign that is spoken against," and that a "sword" would pierce through her own soul. Where-as in Abraham's case another offering was found and Isaac was spared, Mary had to go through the agony of seeing her son crucified before her eyes.

No wonder there is a note of ultimate seriousness about "believing" in the New Testament. It means receiving God's infinitely gracious gift, yes, but it means walking a way of obedience from which there is no turning back. It means Christ in our hearts, but also a cross on our backs. The road leads to life, but it passes first through shame, rejection, and death.

Isn't Mary a pattern for us here? Paul found that being a chosen instrument of God brings with it a strange future: "I will show him how much he must suffer for the sake of my name" (Acts 9:15, 16). In our own time Tom Skinner's receiving Christ by faith meant risking everything by a break with the street gang of which he had been leader. But whatever may lie ahead in an unknown future, a living faith stands ready: "Let it be to me according to your word."

Last of all, Mary is a model for the faithful in her *trust in God's promise*. Elizabeth pronounces this blessing upon her: "Blessed is she who believed that there would be a fulfillment of what was spoken to her from the Lord." Mary had no visible evidence to cling to and no precedent to fall back on. There was no community which could reinforce her faith, nor any dramatic sign from heaven to confirm it. All she had was the word of God's promise, and she believed it. She trusted that God would do the incredible, unheard-of-thing which he had pledged himself to do. This is Christian faith; faith, as Paul puts it, "in the God who raises the dead and calls the things that be not as though they were"; faith that counts the God of heaven and earth to be faithful; faith that holds on at Good Friday and sees Easter come; faith that faces a worldwide task with courage and receives the Spirit at Pentecost.

Maybe this is the light in which we should have seen the Virgin Mary all along. We may well honor and follow her—not as a kind of counter-Christ, but as the first Christian. The key issue is not what Mary means to your faith, but what Mary's faith means to you.

1. Why has the Virgin Mary been given such a prominent role in some expressions of Roman Catholicism? Why do Protestants object to this?
2. From the evidence given by Luke, how would you describe Mary's personality and character?
3. According to the account in Luke, what is the reason for God's choice of Mary? What does this suggest about his choice of us?
4. Is faith possible without some prior revelation of God? Explain your answer.
5. How are obedience and faith related? Which comes first?
6. Up until now, what have been your impressions about the Virgin Mary?

CHRISTMAS PRAISE

Background Scripture—Luke 2:15-20

When the angels went away from them into heaven, the shepherds said to one another, "Let us go over to Bethlehem and see this thing that has happened, which the Lord has made known to us." And they went with haste, and found Mary and Joseph, and the babe lying in a manger. And when they saw it they made known the saying which had been told them concerning this child; and all who heard it wondered at what the shepherds told them. But Mary kept all these things, pondering them in her heart. And the shepherds returned, glorifying and praising God for all they had seen, as it had been told them (Luke 2:15-20).

Praise to God—heaven and earth were full of it on Christmas night. A vast choir of angels sang it in the heavens outside Bethlehem, and the shepherds echoed it when they saw the newborn Savior. "The shepherds returned," writes Luke, "glorifying and praising God for all they had heard and seen, as it had been told them" (2:20).

These shepherds are a pattern for all of us. They show us how the worship of heaven, the praise of the angels, becomes a reality here on earth. They praised God because they had *heard* a message from heaven And what a word it was! "Be not afraid, for behold I bring you good news of great joy which will come to all the people" (2:10). They heard a message of gladness, a word of great joy for all the sons of earth. A Savior was born for the world. He was Christ—God's anointed one, God's Messiah. He was the Lord—Jehovah himself in human form, the God of Abraham, Isaac, and Jacob visiting his people.

Luke always seems to associate praise with a heavenly word. An angel brings a message to Zechariah that his prayer has been heard and his wife will bear a son. When the child is born, Zechariah cries in response, "Blessed be the Lord God of Israel, for he hath visited and redeemed his people" (1:68). Mary receives the grander message of a more wonderful birth. Her reaction to that word is "My soul magnifies the Lord and my spirit rejoices in God my Savior" (1:46. 47). Simeon also was told by divine revelation that he would not see death before he had beheld the Lord's Christ. Later, when he took the infant Jesus in his arms, he "blessed God."

Praise, as we see it in Luke's Gospel, is man's echo to God's gracious word. The Lord speaks in mercy from heaven; man responds with worship on earth. The Most High makes known his promise to men, and they respond with the Amen of faith and praise. That's why Luke can use the word "bless" both as God's action and as man's. On the one hand, God blesses Mary and Mary's child (1:42), but we also read of Simeon that he "blessed God" (2:28). When we "bless the Lord with all that is within us," we are simply offering back to him in thankfulness the blessing which he has first bestowed.

Worship, then, is first of all a matter of listening. Sometimes it is said that preaching has no place in worship, since worship is what men offer to God. But this attitude betrays a serious misunderstanding. If worship were only man's action, it would never become the overflowing praise of the New Testament. Worship is our response to *God's* act. Preaching has a central place in worship precisely because God speaks through his Word when it is proclaimed among his people. When we hear the good news of his love and the great things he has done for us in Christ, then we can respond in true worship.

But, to get back to the shepherds, their praises on Christmas night arose not only from what they heard but also from what they *saw*. The sounds of angel music had scarcely faded in the night sky when the shepherds said to each other, "Let us go over to Bethlehem and see this thing that has happened, which the Lord has made known to us" (2:15). And afterwards they "returned glorifying and praising God for all that they had heard and seen" (2:20). Here again, this is a familiar motif in Luke's Gospel. People are led to praise God because of what they see. The aged Simeon lifts his voice in praise to God, for, he says, "mine eyes have seen thy salvation" (2:30). When Jesus healed the paralyzed man, the onlookers "glorified God and were filled with awe, saying, 'We have seen strange things today'" (5:26). Jesus restored a blind man outside Jericho "and all the people, when they saw it, gave praise to God" (18:43). And finally, as Jesus drew near to Jerusalem at the close of his ministry, "the whole multitude of the disciples began to rejoice and praise God with a loud voice for all the mighty works that they had seen" (19:37).

Here is the glory of the Christmas revelation. It was announced in joyful tidings from heaven, but it didn't stop with words. The Lord of Glory entered into history, at a place that could be visited, in a body that could be seen and touched. Along with the word was the deed; together with the voice came the Living Word. The message from heaven was confirmed by the incarnation on earth. The pattern holds during our Lord's ministry. The word of divine forgiveness (5:20) is followed by the act of divine power (5:24).

The witness of the church grows out of this work of the living God. The apostle John crisply sums it up this way: "That which we have seen and heard we proclaim also to you." And by faith, we today see what they saw: Christ born in lowliness out of love for the world; Christ living and ministering among men, healing, helping, liberating; Christ dying for the sins of all; Christ risen as the victor over death. With eyes of faith, we too behold his glory, "glory as of the only begotten of the Father, full of grace and truth." And beholding him, the Word made flesh, we are moved to praise. "Blessed is the King who comes in the name of the Lord" (19:38).

The Gospel of Luke ends on the same note with which it began. The praise of Christmas is still sounding, now in richer, deeper tones after Good Friday and Easter. The disciples have *heard* afresh God's word, the witness of the risen Christ himself. For "beginning with Moses and all the prophets, he interpreted to them in all the Scriptures the things concerning himself" (24:37). No wonder they asked, "Did not our hearts burn within us while he talked to us on the road, while he opened to us the Scriptures?" But more than this, they learned that now "repentance and forgiveness of sins are to be preached in his name to all nations." They are to be "witnesses of these things" and shall receive the promise of the Father to equip them for their mission (24:47-49). All this they heard, and more. But they also *saw* him. "The Lord is risen indeed and has appeared to Simon" (24:34). Later, as he stood before the gathered group of disciples, "they were startled and frightened and supposed that they saw a spirit." But he said, "See my hands and my feet, that it is I, myself. Handle me and see, for a spirit has not flesh and bones as you see that I have" (24:37-40). And at Bethany, before his ascension, they saw him again, lifting his hands in blessing over them. Then they, like the shepherds, returned with great joy and were continually in the temple blessing God." And from their place of worship they set forth with burning hearts to tell everywhere what they had seen and heard—that the whole world might be filled with his praise. Let it be so for us!

1. *What works and attributes of God especially call forth praise in Luke, chapters 1–2?*
2. *Someone has said that praising God is the highest, purest activity of which human beings are capable. How would you defend that claim?*
3. *What must happen in our lives before we can sincerely praise God?*
4. *What role should our* feelings *play in praising God? Is there value in praising God even when we "don't feel like it?"*
5. *We have not heard Christ speak, nor have we seen him with our eyes. Can our faith be as real as that of his first disciples? Explain your answer.*
6. *At what time in your life have you been most moved to praise God?*

5

FOR THE BROKENHEARTED

Background Scripture—Luke 3:1-14

In the fifteenth year of the reign of Tiberius Caesar, Pontius Pilate being governor of Judea, and Herod being tetrarch of Galilee, and his brother Philip tetrarch of the region of Ituraea and Trachonitis, and Lysanias tetrarch of Abilene, in the high-priesthood of Annas and Caiaphas, the word of God came to John the son of Zechariah in the wilderness; and he went into all the region about the Jordan, preaching a baptism of repentance for the forgiveness of sins. As it is written in the book of the words of Isaiah the prophet, "The voice of one crying in the wilderness; Prepare the way of the Lord, make his paths straight. Every valley shall be filled, and every mountain and hill shall be brought low, and the crooked shall be made straight, and the rough ways shall be made smooth; and all flesh shall see the salvation of God." He said therefore to the multitudes that came out to be baptized by him, "You brood of vipers! Who warned you to flee from the wrath to come? Bear fruits that befit repentance, and do not begin to say to yourselves, 'We have Abraham as our father'; for I tell you, God is able from these stones to raise up children to Abraham. Even now the axe is laid to the root of the trees; every tree therefore that does not bear good fruit is cut down and thrown into the fire" (Luke 3:1-9).

You might call it "the Gospel of the brokenhearted"—Luke deals so much with *repentance*. He shares with Matthew and Mark the report that John and

Jesus preached repentance, but he adds much more which neither of the other evangelists records. Only Luke has John the Baptist citing in detail the "fruits that befit repentance" (3:8-14). To Jesus' announcement, "I came not to call the righteous but sinners," Luke alone adds the words "to repentance" (5:32). These sober words of Jesus (when discussing certain fatal accidents) are found only in Luke's Gospel, "Unless you repent you will all likewise perish" (13:3, 5). Repentance is described three times in Luke 15 as man's great need and the occasion of heaven's rejoicing. For Luke, repentance, together with the forgiveness of sins, sums up the message which Jesus said should be preached in his name to all nations (24:47). In all, the third evangelist has roughly twice as many references to repentance as Matthew and Mark put together.

Well, what does Luke mean by "repentance"? Like most other biblical writers, he is not concerned to give definitions. We search his writings in vain for any systematic treatment of theological terms. Actually, however, he gives us something far better. Luke shows us, through persons with whom Jesus dealt and through parables which he told, how repentance works. Here is repentance in action—and its opposite. Look, for example, at the woman who washed Jesus' feet with her tears and wiped them with the hairs of her head. That is repentance. Here was a deep self-humbling, a brokenness of heart. Here was an extravagant outpouring of devotion and gratitude. "Her sins," said Jesus, "which are many are forgiven, for she loved much" (7:47). Luke shows us another example of a repentant sinner in his account of the crucifixion. Apparently this man had first joined his companion in railing at Jesus, but as time went on a change came over him. He rebuked the blasphemer on the opposite cross, confessing that the punishment which society was meting out to them was only just. Then, acknowledging his own guilt, he committed himself in trust to the dying Savior beside him. "Jesus, remember me when you come in your kingly power" (23:42).

Luke also includes two parables in which Jesus illustrates what repentance is. A younger son demands his share of the property and goes into a far country to squander it. There, debauched, impoverished, and lonely, he comes to himself and thinks of his father's house. "I will arise and go to my father and I will say to him, 'Father, I have sinned against heaven and before you and am no longer worthy to be called your son. Treat me as one of your hired servants'" (15:18-19). And so he returns to his father, humbled, brokenhearted, yet trusting that he will be received. Or think of the tax collector in that unforgettable temple scene. He stands afar off; he will not even lift up his eyes heavenward. All he can do is beat his breast and say, "God be merciful to me a sinner" (18:13).

Now, it is striking that all four of these passages occur only in Luke, the Gospel that majors in repentance. These, as Luke sees them, are pictures from life of the way in which we ought to respond to the grace that comes to us in Jesus Christ.

But this is only half the story. For every broken heart that Luke portrays there is another that is decidedly unbroken. Along with each repentant sinner there appears another who has missed the meaning of repentance completely. In the account of the weep-

ing, penitent woman we meet also Simon the Pharisee. He entertains Jesus in his home but shows him
no special courtesies, no warmth of affection. He
looks on the woman's contrition with scorn and re-
pugnance and becomes highly suspicious of Jesus for
accepting it. Then there is the other criminal on the
cross, the one who lashes out at everyone around
him. He shows no sense of guilt, no fear of God. His
bitter mockery to the very end, is "Are you not the
Christ? Save yourself and us" (23:39).

In the parables, too, this same counterpart appears. The returning son has an elder brother. The
latter has never wandered to a far country, but he is
desperately estranged from the father's heart. In
pained self-righteousness he pleads against his father's
generosity. To him, the returning prodigal is not "my
brother" but "this son of yours." The younger boy
got much more than he deserved and he knew it, but
this son was persuaded that he had received less than
his deserts—and it made him miserable.

In the last of these scenes, the Pharisee stands con-
fidently in the temple which the tax collector hardly
dares approach. He recites his virtues smugly before
God—and an imposing list of them he has. But his
prayer betrays no sense of need, no realization of
grace. It is poisoned through and through by his contempt for those whom he considers beneath him.
They are less orthodox than he, or perhaps less concerned about social issues. Here is one more spirit
that has never been humbled, one more heart that
has never known breaking. Jesus came to call sinners
to repentance, and these are men who still need desperately to hear his call.

Can we discern a few common elements in these

29

narratives? Among the penitent, we see confession of lostness and guilt, together with a yearning cry for mercy. Above all, they show an awareness that in Jesus, God has drawn near to men in grace. In him, forgiveness and hope are to be found, and to him each penitent sinner owes everything. On the other hand, repentance is decidedly absent where there is no sense of personal unworthiness, where there is a tendency to look down on others, and where God is looked on as a debtor rather than as a savior. And how different are the results! For those who scorn repentance—a sulking mood, a loveless spirit, a shameful abasing, and a hopeless death. But for the penitent—joy abounding, a new power for loving, a lifting up of head and heart, and life forever in the presence of Christ.

The key is to grasp who Jesus is and why he came. It is to see ourselves in his light instead of comparing ourselves with others. Repentance is a profound change of mind in which we see God, ourselves, and others in an entirely new way. It arises within us when we realize that God in Christ is our gracious Savior and that we are the wandering, alienated, guilty ones who need saving. It is the change in which we stop saying, "Give me the share of property that falls to me" and begin to say, "I am no longer worthy to be called your son." It means that a man stops lauding his virtues and begins confessing his guilt, stops demanding justice and begins calling for mercy.

That is genuine repentance, and where it is present, the fruits which John the Baptist demanded begin to appear. Those who have much are ready to share with those who lack. Businessmen are just in their dealings, and men with authority cease to intimidate and extort. Repentance leads to changed living and loving action. But these are the fruits, not the root. What Luke makes piercingly plain is that all such acts without a contrite spirit may be no more than the elder brother's "Pay me!" or the Pharisee's parade. There is no substitute for a broken heart.

1. *How would you define repentance?*
2. *Why is repentance a necessity for entrance into God's kingdom?*
3. *Is "feeling sorry for what you've done" the same as repentance? Explain.*
4. *How does repentance affect our attitudes toward God? Toward others? Toward ourselves?*
5. *If you wanted to lead another person to repentance, how would you go about it?*
6. *How has repentance involved a "change of mind" in your life?*

THE SPIRIT-CONTROLLED LIFE

Background Scripture—Luke 4:1-19

And he came to Nazareth, where he had been brought up; and he went to the synagogue, as his custom was, on the sabbath day. And he stood up to read; and there was given to him the book of the prophet Isaiah. He opened the book and found the place where it was written, "The Spirit of the Lord is upon me, because he has anointed me to preach good news to the poor. He has sent me to proclaim release to the captives and recovering of sight to the blind, to set at liberty those who are oppressed, to proclaim the acceptable year of the Lord" (Luke 4:16-19).

The minister's wife, with some perplexity and a touch of annoyance, interrupted the guest Bible study leader with these words: "I can understand God the Father and Jesus, but why do we have to have this Spirit?"

Perhaps Dr. Luke had some such question in mind when he wrote his Gospel. More than any other Gospel writer, he highlights the role of the Holy Spirit in the life and ministry of Jesus. In the first four chapters alone he includes more references to the Holy Spirit than are found in Matthew's entire Gospel and twice as many as are found in Mark. Luke's is the Gospel of the Spirit-controlled life.

The ministry of the Spirit first becomes evident in the circumstances surrounding Jesus' birth. John the

Baptist, forerunner of our Lord, is to be "filled with the Holy Spirit even from his mother's womb." Elizabeth is "filled with the Holy Spirit" when she testifies to the blessedness of Mary's child, as is Zechariah when he foretells the coming salvation (1:67). Simeon is taught and inspired by the Spirit as he rejoices over the infant Jesus (2:26-28). Most important, our Savior's miraculous birth itself is attributed to the direct agency of the Holy Spirit: "And the angel said to her, the Holy Spirit will come upon you and the power of the Most High will overshadow you; therefore the child to be born will be called holy, the Son of God" (1:35).

Luke shares with Matthew, Mark, and John the record that the Holy Spirit descended upon Jesus at the time of his baptism and later led him into the wilderness where he was tempted by the devil. It is Luke alone, however, who notes that Jesus was "full of the Holy Spirit" after his baptism and that he returned after his temptations "in the power of the Holy Spirit" (4:1, 14). Luke wants to emphasize that from the very beginning of our Lord's ministry he was constantly guided and empowered by the Spirit of God.

This was a matter, Luke tells us, of which Jesus was fully conscious. When he stood up in the synagogue at Nazareth to read from the prophet Isaiah, he deliberately chose this passage: "The Spirit of the Lord is upon me because he has anointed me to preach good news to the poor, he has sent me to proclaim release to the captives and recovering of sight to the blind, to set at liberty those who are oppressed, to proclaim the acceptable year of the Lord" (4:18, 19). In proclaiming to his countrymen that these words were now fulfilled, Jesus was both describing what he had come to do and also claiming to be himself God's Messiah, God's anointed one, the one on whom God had set his Spirit. Luke is giving us here a background for everything else in his Gospel. All of the preaching, healing, liberating ministry of Jesus Christ roots in one great affirmation: "The Spirit of the Lord is upon me."

This work of the Spirit in Jesus, as it appears in Luke's Gospel, involves more than the power to perform certain tasks. Even the thoughts and feelings of our Lord are charged with the Spirit's life-giving power. Upon hearing of the fruitful ministry of his followers, for example, Jesus "rejoiced in the Holy Spirit" (10:21).

Some may find this emphasis in Luke rather disturbing—at least at first glance. "What about the deity of Christ?" someone objects. "If Christ is truly God in the flesh, he can do all these things in his own power. Why must he depend upon the Holy Spirit?"

The answer to that question leads us into one of Luke's most significant emphases. Though he believes with every other New Testament writer that Jesus is the unique Son of God, Luke lays great stress upon his "humanness." The Jesus of Luke's Gospel is the ideal Man. He is all that a man ought to be, the perfect Exemplar of the human race. And as true man, he lives his life and fulfills his calling as we are meant to do. Jesus shows us, in the words of the confused minister's wife, "why we have to have this Spirit." He, the Spirit-controlled Man, is the pattern and prophecy of what his followers are to become.

Now we can see why Luke gives special attention to the work of the Spirit in Jesus. Remember that he is writing, along with his Gospel, the Book of Acts. That latter book is the thrilling story of the acts of the Holy Spirit in the early Church. After Pentecost, Luke tells us, believers were filled, guided, and empowered by the Holy Spirit for their witness and service in Christ's name. There are some seventy references in the Book of Acts alone to the activity of the Spirit of God in the Christian community. What Luke does in his Gospel, accordingly, is to show that all this had its beginning in the life and ministry of Jesus. He is the Messiah, the anointed one, and believers have come to share in his anointing. The same Spirit who dwelt without measure in him now dwells in his followers. The secret of his Messianic ministry is now the open secret of theirs.

But the connection is even closer than that. Not only do believers share in the heavenly anointing of their Lord, but it is he himself, the risen one, who sends the Spirit upon them. Remember his words at the close of Luke's Gospel: "You are witnesses of these things, and behold I send the promise of my Father upon you. But stay in the city until you are clothed with power from on high" (24:49). Note that: "I send the promise of my Father." The Holy Spirit comes to us *from Christ*. The Spirit brings to us the life of the living Lord and enables us to follow in his way.

Jesus had hinted even during his earthly ministry that this provision would be made for his church: "When they bring you before the synagogues and the rulers and authorities," he counseled, "do not be anxious how or what you are to answer or what you are to say, for the Holy Spirit will teach you in that very hour what you ought to say" (12:11, 12). In other words, the same Spirit who gave heavenly wisdom and boldness to our Lord will supply the need of his embattled servants.

What an encouragement for the people of God! The Spirit at work in the Head is also at work in the members of the body. The life which he lived as the Pioneer and Perfecter of our faith is now a possibility—indeed a promise—for us. As he, the Son of God from all eternity, was led by the Spirit, so now are we, the sons of God through faith, directed by the same Spirit. Paul put it just so: "As many as are led by the Spirit of God, they are the sons of God."

But we find more here than encouragement; the Spirit-controlled life of Jesus is a model and challenge for us, too. Luke makes it plain that though we are to expect and rely upon the gift of the Holy Spirit, we are never to take his presence for granted. When speaking to his followers about persistent prayer and about God's faithfulness in hearing it, Jesus concluded with this: "If you then who are evil know how to give good gifts to your children, how much more will the heavenly Father give the Holy Spirit to those who ask him" (11:13). *Ask* for the promised Spirit. The gathered disciples continued in prayer in the upper room even after Jesus assured them that the Spirit would be given. His promise, in other words, was not a cushion to recline on but a call to believing prayer. May it be that for us!

1. *Luke 1:15 says that John the Baptist was to be filled with the Spirit from birth. How is it that the*

Holy Spirit descended on Jesus at the time of his
baptism—when he was about thirty years old?

2. According to Luke 4:18-19, what was the central
activity for which the Spirit anointed Jesus? How
does this relate to accounts of the Spirit's working through believers in the Book of Acts?

3. If the Spirit was guiding and controlling his life,
was Jesus passive in the process? How does the
Spirit's filling differ, in its effects upon the person,
from demonic possession?

4. What does it mean to be "filled" with the Spirit?
Can this happen more than once in a person's life?

5. In what ways can you identify the Spirit's working
in your life?

7

FOR ALL PEOPLES

Background Scripture—Luke 4:25-29

*"But in truth, I tell you, there were many
widows in Israel in the days of Elijah, when the
heaven was shut up three years and six months,
when there came a great famine over all the
land; and Elijah was sent to none of them but
only to Zarephath, in the land of Sidon, to a
woman who was a widow. And there were
many lepers in Israel in the time of the prophet
Elisha; and none of them was cleansed, but only
Naaman the Syrian." When they heard this, all
in the synagogue were filled with wrath. And
they rose up and put him out of the city and led
him to the brow of the hill on which their city
was built, that they might throw him down
headlong (Luke 4:25-29).*

"We all tend to hear the Great Commission *selectively*." This was the incisive comment of a speaker
at a recent U.S. Congress on Evangelism. He pointed
out how the early church had missed the full meaning of the risen Lord's command. When Jesus said,
"You shall be my witnesses in Jerusalem and in all
Judea and in Samaria, and unto the uttermost parts
of the earth," the first Christians heard that to mean
all *Jews* in those places. In fact, it later took visions
and special revelations to convince Peter and others
that the Gentiles were included in the plan. And
hasn't the church in our time often had the same
problem? Some of us hear it like this: "Go and make
disciples among all middle-class Americans." Others

hear it as "Go and preach the Gospel to people at least a thousand miles away." Very few take it to mean all people, everywhere.

Surely one of the best antidotes for this affliction is a careful study of Luke's Gospel. One of the things we notice from the outset is its worldwide perspective. Aged Simeon speaks of God's salvation which he "has prepared in the presence of all people; a light for revelation to the Gentiles and for glory to thy people Israel" (2:30-32). Luke writes of John the Baptist's ministry as fulfilling the word of Isaiah, "All flesh shall see the salvation of God" (3:6). Whereas Matthew begins his genealogy of Jesus with Abraham, Luke carries it all the way back to Adam, showing the relation of our Lord to the whole human race. Luke records also the word of Jesus that "men shall come from east and west and from north and south and sit at the table in the kingdom of God" (13:29). And he gives the commission and purpose of the risen Lord in these words: "that repentance and forgiveness of sins should be preached in his name to all nations" (24:47).

The keen edge of this Gospel strikes at the very root of all the hedges that men have erected against each other. Here is a message devastating to exclusiveness, prejudice, and the respect of persons. People lived in our Lord's time with many of the same distinctions that we are aware of today—those of nationality, race, religious custom, social class, and economic status. But Luke pictures Jesus Christ as one who in his ministry cut across all these lines of distinction and smashed these barriers down.

The rich, for example, have often been inclined to hold the poor in contempt. God, however, chose

Mary, a handmaiden of low estate (1:48). She sings of how God puts down the mighty and exalts those of low degree; how he fills the hungry with good things and sends the rich away empty (1:52-53). And Jesus himself pronounces a special blessing on the poor: "Blessed are you poor, for yours is the kingdom of God." He makes it clear that the poor beggar, Lazarus, is comforted in the life to come (16:22).

In the culture of our Lord's time, women were regarded by men as distinctly inferior. It was a regular part of the Jewish liturgy for men to praise God that they were not born as women. But the Lord of glory was born of a woman and allowed himself to be dependent on female support (8:1-3). He is seen ministering to a widow (7:12), comforting one who comes to him for healing and accepting the grateful penitence of one who has fallen (7:47-48). Jesus praises the concern of Mary to sit at his feet and hear his word (10:42). And at the last it is the multitude of women who lament him, who stand by him at the cross, and are first at his tomb.

Think also of how the Jews looked down on the Samaritans as an inferior, corrupted, half-breed race. Jesus, on the contrary, by deliberate design went through Samaria (9:52). And in one of the most famous parables ever told, he made a nameless foreigner the hero. We call him "The Good Samaritan."

And what of the attitudes held by the Pharisees? They scorned the "people of the land," the "sinners," the tax collectors, and all others who paid little attention to the Law. But this disturbing Jesus receives sinners and eats with them (15:2). He goes to the house of a tax collector (19:5). He is known as the friend of such people (7:34), and even calls some of them to be his disciples (5:27).

The point here is not that Jesus was against the rich, the male, the Jew, or the Pharisee. He loved the Jewish people and saw them as his first responsibility. On at least three occasions he dined with Pharisees. All those whom he called to be his special disciples were men, and he was buried, you remember, by a rich man in the man's own tomb. His love extended, in other words, to every "in" group. But Luke's special emphasis lies elsewhere. He shows us Jesus as going out of his way to stand with those who are despised, discriminated against, laughed at, or regarded as inferior. Jesus goes further than that. He indicates that from God's point of view the tables are often turned. The Jews will reject the Gospel and it will be given to the Gentiles (14:16; 20:9). The Jewish Levite and priest fail to show compassion, but the Samaritan loves. The nine lepers, who are presumably Jews, forget to give thanks, but not the grateful Samaritan. Those publicans and harlots so despised by the religious elite go into the kingdom of God before the Pharisees. Women stand by Jesus loyally when the men have forsaken him, and Lazarus, the poor man, is in Abraham's bosom while the self-indulgent rich man is in a place of torment. How things change!

What happened as a result? How did the nationalist, the strict Pharisee, the rich man react to this kind of person and this teaching? Notice what happened in Jesus' home town. After he had reminded his hearers that Elijah was sent not to Jewish widows, but to one in the area of Sidon, and how God used Elisha to cleanse Naaman the hated Syrian, the people in the synagogue were "filled with wrath and sought to kill him" (4:25-29). When he told the parable of the wicked husbandman whom the master replaced, the scribes and chief priests "tried to lay hands on him." In the end, the best people of his day reviled him as the "friend of publicans and sinners" and plotted to destroy him.

We find it easy to react with righteous indignation against these Pharisees and other Christ-opposers. "How heartless and blind can you get?" we ask. But what if someone came into our all-white churches and began an all-out effort to welcome the blacks of the community into the fellowship? What if someone came into our largely middle-class churches and urged that we concentrate the resources of the church upon winning the poor? And what if someone came into our staunch one-nationality churches and sparked a movement to join with Christians of another culture? Would he raise a storm?

How do we stand, really, in the searching light of this worldwide Gospel, this barrier-blasting good news of God? Are we for the most part a self-satisfied middle-class church, tending to look down with righteous indignation on the nonworkers and social dropouts? Are we still proud of our separateness, suspicious of other denominations and Christian traditions? And do we remain for the most part a white church, extremely reluctant to receive black people or those of other minority groups?

We claim that we want to be Christ's, but are we really happy with his outlook? We want to be biblical, but have we truly heard this message from the Scriptures? Will we seek the black man, the minority-group members, the poor, the deprived, as eagerly and as constantly as we seek for fine new members of "our kind"?

What we have failed to grasp is the "must" of God's purpose. This worldwide, universal reach of the Gospel is his design. And because we have missed it, in our pessimism and half belief, we have missed also his wonderful surprise. This kind of ministry will not be, as some fear, the *death* of our churches, but rather th*e life* of them, because the living Lord is out ahead of us, leading us on. What he looks for in us is a determination to take his Gospel for just what it is: the Gospel for all peoples.

1. *How has your church, or how have you, "heard the Great Commission selectively?"*
2. *What are the chief barriers that divide people in your community? In your church?*
3. *In what practical ways can Christians today follow Jesus in "stepping across" lines of division?*
4. *What sort of opposition is directed today against people who try to do this?*
5. *What does it mean to be "all things to all men?" How can we maintain our identity, our uniqueness, and still be accepting of others?*
6. *What about world government? Is that an answer to some of the divisions among nations and peoples?*

8

THE GRACIOUS GUEST

Background Scripture—Luke 5:29-32

> *And Levi made him a great feast in his house;
> and there was a large company of tax collectors
> and others sitting at table with them. And the
> Pharisees and their scribes murmured against
> his disciples, saying, "Why do you eat and drink
> with tax collectors and sinners?" And Jesus
> answered them, "Those who are well have no
> need of a physician, but those who are sick; I
> have not come to call the righteous, but sinners
> to repentance" (Luke 5:29-32).*

"Every man is like the company he is wont to
keep." Do you believe that? The axiom goes all the
way back to Euripides, a Greek dramatist in the fifth
century B.C. For many, it speaks a wisdom not to be
challenged. Another old saying puts it more concise-
ly: "Birds of a feather flock together." Find out about
those whom a man befriends, runs the argument, and
you have found the measure of the man.

Strange, then, isn't it, that Jesus Christ often gathered with such a disreputable, unpromising group of
people? He wasn't at all particular about whom he
ate with! The popular talk about him was, "This man
receives sinners and eats with them" (15:2). Everyone knew that he had attended a great feast at the
home of Levi, the tax collector, with a number of
Levi's cronies (5:29). If there was any practice at
that time which would correspond with, say, eating

with Mafia chieftains today, that was it. Jesus had even gone to dine with one of the most notorious men in Palestine, Zacchaeus of Jericho. Were not the religious authorities justified in concluding that Jesus must be a man of dubious character himself? It seemed disgraceful. Claiming to be some kind of a rabbi, he could sit at table with the worst riffraff in town—eating, talking, laughing with the worst of them. There must be something wrong with this Nazarene, they reasoned. Why else would a man keep company with people like that?

Yes, that was the question—why else? That's the question that challenges the old sayings. The most profound issue is not who a man's associates are, but *why* he seeks them out. When Jesus was challenged about his practice ("Why do you eat and drink with tax collectors and sinners?"), he was ready with an answer. "Those who are well have no need of a physician, but those who are sick. I have not come to call the righteous but sinners to repentance" (5:30-32). He was with the least and the lowest, the wicked and the worst, because he came to heal and save them. So he went where they were. This was the thing his contemporaries couldn't understand. Good men, godly men, rarely had anything to do with such people. Perhaps the best of Israel's religious leaders would have tried to help the abandoned and the despised if such persons had come seeking help, with proper contrition. But for a man to go to the haunts of evildoers, to the homes of sinners, even to eat with them —there was no precedent for that. When it came to black sheep, there simply were no other seeking shepherds. No wonder people misunderstood him!

Was Jesus, then, a spokesman for the despised

classes, a kind of first-century revolutionary leader with no time for conventional society? No, somehow he doesn't fit that mold. Luke shows us that on at least three occasions he went to eat in the home of a Pharisee (7:36, 11:37, 14:1)! Here he is associating with dignitaries, with the religious elite of Israel. Perhaps there were some among the outcasts, the "people of the land," who criticized him for this: "See how he frequents the homes of the important people" or, "I hear that Jesus is hob-nobbing with these self-righteous Pharisees now." And there was no doubt about these accusations. He was frequently at a Pharisee's table.

But once again the question comes—Why? Did he feel the need to curry favor with them? Were they his kind of people? Hardly. He made little attempt to please the Pharisees, far less to show that his religious position was similar to theirs. In fact, on more than one occasion he roundly denounced them and made them fiercely angry. But in spite of all this he did not decline their invitations. Whenever welcomed, he dined in their homes. Why?

Luke notes how on each occasion Jesus made use of his visit in a Pharisee's home to teach a much-needed lesson. He taught Simon the Pharisee that the secret of real devotion to God is an awareness of "how great our sins and miseries are" and how free and full is God's forgiveness (7:47). He taught another Pharisee that outward washings are no sign of inner purity (11:37 ff.). Again, while dining at the home of a ruler, he showed the Pharisees how ridiculous it was to condemn an act of healing on the Sabbath day (14:1ff.). In these homes, also, there were sinners whom he summoned to repentance. He loved

46

them, too—loved them too much to leave them secure in their lifeless formalism. That is why he sat at table with Pharisees.

But these are not the only homes at which Jesus appears in Luke's Gospel. He dines with publicans and Pharisees to win and teach them, but he also comes as a guest to the homes of loyal followers. He gladly visits those who choose "the good portion" and listen at his feet (10:38-42). And on the night in which he has betrayed, we see him in a large supper room, dining with his disciples. There, around a table he institutes the Lord's Supper (22:14 ff.).

Why does Luke show us all these table scenes from our Lord's earthly ministry? For one thing, Jesus appears here as a man among men, entering fully into the common life of those for whom he came. But the significance of this is more than historical. Luke also records a postresurrection appearance which indicates that table scenes have meaning for the Church's life today. Jesus draws near to the men on the Emmaus road and opens the Scriptures to them. When they approach the village, he apparently plans to continue his journey, but they urge him to stay with them, and he accepts. While they are at table, he blesses the bread, breaks it, and gives it to them. In that hour they recognize who he is; he is "known to them in the breaking of the bread." Jesus must have had a charactristic way of giving thanks and distributing the food. These Emmaus disciples had seen him do it before. Everything suddenly fell into place when they saw him at table. They knew then that it was he.

Luke is obviously saying something here about the place of the Lord's Supper in the Christian community. When we meet in Christ's name, sharing in the supper which he instituted, his presence among us becomes very real. For us, however, the celebration of the Lord's Supper has become a relatively infrequent and highly formal occasion. The message of Luke's table scenes has a much more domestic, everyday flavor than we usually associate with Communion. The message is that Jesus Christ, the living Lord, delights to share the common life of his people. Where his presence is sought, where his word is welcomed, he himself is present—present at the center of family life—present when we gather about our tables. Not only on special sacramental occasions but in the ordinary routine of domestic life, Jesus is known in the breaking of the bread. No tables are too humble, no homes too unworthy, for this gracious guest.

1. *Think of the people with whom you most frequently associate. Why do you choose to be with them?*
2. *How much should your choice of associates be influenced by "what people will think?"*
3. *If you are a Christian, is it possible to have a close friend who is not? Defend your answer.*
4. *What is the religious significance (for Christians) of a family meal?*
5. *Jesus customarily dined in homes to which he was invited. Can you think of an instance in Luke in which he "invited himself" to someone's home? What significance do you see in that?*

9

GOING WITH CHRIST

Background Scripture—Luke 9:51-62

> As they were going along the road, a man
> said to him, "I will follow you wherever you
> go." And Jesus said to him, "Foxes have holes,
> and birds of the air have nests; but the Son of
> man has nowhere to lay his head." To another
> he said, "Follow me." But he said, "Lord, let
> me first go and bury my father." But he said to
> him, "Leave the dead to bury their own dead;
> but as for you, go and proclaim the kingdom of
> God." Another said, "I will follow you, Lord;
> but let me first say farewell to those at my
> home." Jesus said to him, "No one who puts
> his hand to the plow and looks back is fit for
> the kingdom of God" (Luke 9:57-62).

One of the great distinctives of Luke's Gospel is
his message of "the Way." The massive central section, 9:51–19:44 (which contains most of the ma-
terial that is peculiarly Lukan), is all set in the frame-
work of a *journey*. Jesus is traveling toward Jerusalem (9:51, 53; 13:22; 17:11; 18:31; 19:21). Time
and again it is mentioned that he is "on the road" or
"passing through" various towns and villages.

For Luke, however, the significance of this journey
is more than geographical. There are very few references to specific sites along the route. The journey
motif, into which a wealth of teaching is woven, has
a deeper meaning. It depicts a journey of faith and
obedience along which Christians are to follow their
Lord.

Notice the point at which the journey begins. The self-revelation of the Savior to his disciples has now reached its climax. They have confessed him as the Christ of God (9:20) and have beheld his unveiled glory on the Mount of Transfiguration (9:28 ff.). They have been clearly told that suffering, rejection, death, and resurrection are ahead for him.

As Luke puts it, "The days drew near for him to be received up" (9:51). Here the full saving work of Jesus, culminating in his ascension, is described in the phrase "to be received up." As God's hour was about to strike, the Savior "set his face to go to Jerusalem" (9:51). This phrase, to set one's face, implies a fixed purpose, the firm resolve of one who faces danger or difficulty. Jesus sets himself on a course from which there is no turning back. Luke stresses the fact that this iron determination was too apparent for anyone to miss. In the Samaritan village where the disciples seek to prepare his way, Jesus is not welcomed, because it is so evident that he is headed for Jerusalem. "If he is that closely identified with Jerusalem and its worship," the Samaritans seem to say, "we want no part of him."

This was the path the Savior chose to walk—rejected in Samaria because he was headed for a deeper rejection in Jerusalem. But in spite of all, he cared for those who refused him. James and John wanted to play Elijah all over again, calling down avenging fire from heaven, but Jesus rebuked these "Sons of Thunder." They were ready to destroy, but he came to save.

Notice how Luke says "he *turned* and rebuked them." We often read of Jesus *turning* to speak to the multitude that followed him. In this passage he must turn about even to speak to his disciples. Luke gives us a picture of the Savior striding ahead of his disciples, eyes fixed on his goal. He walks a solitary way.

The way of the Christian is a way which Christ walks before him. The very next incident brings that pattern into clear focus. "As they were going along the road a man said to him, "I will follow you wherever you go." Here is a would-be disciple, an eager volunteer. He would like to walk in the way. Surely Jesus will accept such an offer with enthusiasm! Why, this man is ready for all-out commitment!

But our Lord is not so sure. He wants the man to know exactly what he's getting into. Does he know that this way will be a way of sorrow and death? Does he know anything of his own weakness and instability? "Foxes have holes," says our Lord, "and birds of the air have nests, but the Son of Man has nowhere to lay his head." The Savior finds no certain resting place. The clamant needs of some and the rejection of others keep him moving from town to town. Following him, in other words, means radical insecurity. Is this volunteer, this would-be church member, ready for that? Let a man think this over carefully before he swears allegiance.

To a second wayfarer Jesus says, "Follow me." But the man responds, "Lord, let me first go and bury my father." Now obviously the father had not already died or the man would have been in the midst of funeral preparations at that moment. He probably means that his father is old and feeble and he doesn't wish to leave him in that condition.

But Jesus seems very stern. "Leave the dead to bury their own dead, but as for you, go and proclaim

51

the kingdom of God." Apparently following Jesus is such an urgent matter that it must take priority even over the closest of family ties. To come behind Jesus is life's supreme calling, its number one priority. When his call comes, there is nothing else that anyone needs to do *first*. Others who have not heard this call may be free to do other things, but the disciple is a man under orders. The Lord's business won't wait.

The third man whom Jesus meets along the way offers to come behind him—under certain conditions. "I will follow you, Lord, but let me first say farewell to those at my home." Here again, he wants to do something else *first*. Our Lord never condemned a concern for loved ones and friends, of course, but he refused to let this or anything else claim priority over his call. There can be no true following of him with "strings attached."

Jesus doesn't say to him, "No, you can't go back home." He simply says, "No one who puts his hand to the plow and looks back is fit for the kingdom of God." You can't plow a straight furrow unless you keep your eyes straight ahead. Neither can a man follow Christ with half his heart. He cannot stay close to his Master if he allows anything else to distract him. Discipleship involves total devotion, unconditional loyalty.

These words, severe as they are, can be understood only when we see them in their setting. It is the Jesus who has set his face to go to Jerusalem who makes these demands. He is the one who has chosen the path of homelessness, with no secure resting place. It is he who severs whatever ties would keep him from accomplishing his mission. He, Jesus, is the one whom nothing can distract and who refuses to look back. For his people to *follow* him, therefore, means precisely that. The way to which he calls us is simply the path which he has walked first. His unswerving course provides the inspiration and challenge for ours. Real Christianity means "setting your face" toward God's mission. Oswald Hoffmann sums up the issue in this terse charge to all would-be followers: "Get with Christ, and go with him!"

1. What is the significance for Luke of Christ's "journey to Jerusalem"?
2. Do you get the impression from this passage that Christ discouraged "volunteers"? Discuss this. Why did he seem cool toward their offers?
3. How does following Christ affect loyalty to one's family and friends?
4. How could a person tell if he was "looking back" —failing to give priority to Christ in his life?
5. Can you think of instances in which following Christ may mean walking alone? Discuss these.

"HE COULDN'T CARE MORE"

Background Scripture—Luke 10:25-37

"But a Samaritan, as he journeyed, came to where he was; and when he saw him, he had compassion, and went to him and bound up his wounds, pouring on oil and wine; then he set him on his own beast and brought him to an inn, and took care of him. And the next day he took out two denarii and gave them to the innkeeper, saying, 'Take care of him; and whatever more you spend, I will repay you when I come back.' Which of these three do you think, proved neighbor to the man who fell among the robbers?" He said, "The one who showed mercy on him." And Jesus said to him, "Go and do likewise" (Luke 10:33-37).

From beginning to end, it is a Gospel of compassion. The very first chapters celebrate "the tender mercy of our God" (1:78), and at its close Jesus is praying for his murderers, "Father, forgive them" (23:34). He introduces his ministry as one long career of compassion, preaching good news to the poor, proclaiming release to the captives and recovering of sight to the blind, and setting at liberty those who are oppressed (4:18). And this is only what one would expect, for Jesus comes in the name of the Most High, who is "kind to the ungrateful and the selfish" (6:35). Jesus has compassion on a heart-broken widow who has just lost her only son (7:12-14). He stops to heal a blind beggar who cries, "Jesus, son of David, have mercy on me" (18:37). He cares about a suffering criminal and gives him comfortable words to die by, "Truly I say to you, today you will be with me in paradise" (23:43).

Our word *compassion* hardly does justice to all this. It actually translates a Greek word which is far stronger. We call it "tender mercies," but what is really being talked about is a veritable "pain of love," an anguish of concern. You might say about the one who has compassion that "he couldn't care more." This is the heart of Luke's Gospel. It's all about a Savior who cared so much that it broke his heart and led him to a cross.

On the pages of the same Gospel we read of others who did not seem to care at all, to whom compassion was a thing unknown. They watched Jesus with narrowing eyes "to see whether he would heal on the Sabbath so that they might find an accusation against him" (6:7). They loaded other men with burdens hard to bear, though they would not lift a finger to carry those same burdens themselves (11:46). They were indignant when Jesus' compassion cut across their customary ways (13:14). There were rich men like Dives who feasted sumptuously every day and cared nothing for starving Lazarus at the door. And there were pseudo-religionists who made a pretense of prayer while they gobbled up the inheritance of widows. Our Lord's genuine compassion found rough going in a world like that. It costs something to care.

This way of compassion, we learn from Jesus, is one along which he wants us to follow him. It is striking that the first parable he told after he had set his face to go to Jerusalem was a story about another man on a journey—a man who "had compassion" (10:33). In a way that has charmed and moved and shamed the world ever since, Jesus portrayed in the Good Samaritan a man who truly cares. If you want to discover the ingredients of compassion, take a long look at what this nameless foreigner did. First he showed a certain kind of *vision*. The Samaritan saw the bleeding form by the wayside. At first glance there is nothing remarkable about that. The priest and the Levite saw him, too (10:31, 32). And when they saw him, they quickly passed by on the other side. One glimpse was enough for them. They were careful not to get near enough to see any more. But the Samaritan saw something that attracted him, that drew him. He saw suffering and need, and he couldn't take his eyes off that man until he had done something. Many of us, like the priest and the Levite, don't see because we don't want to see. It's more pleasant to drive around through the nice sections of town than through the slums. It's more comfortable not to look at the sordid problems of poor and forgotten people. But what we are so quick to avoid, compassion looks for and finds. If reporters have a nose for news, then Good Samaritans have eyes for the needy.

But compassion takes a lot more than seeing. There are many times when it demands raw physical *courage*. The priest and the Levite were doubtless kindly and benevolent men, wishing everyone well. But here a man was lying half dead by the roadside, and the men who had done him in were probably still lurking nearby. And we all know that people who meddle in matters like these sometimes get themselves into serious trouble. The priest and the Levite were detouring around real danger. But the Samaritan, though he may have been less prudent, was a good deal more courageous. He took the risks and did what had to be done. Funny how, in the Greek language, the word for compassion is related to the visceral organs. In any language, it seems to take "guts" to show compassion, especially when you are walking down a lonely road.

You know something else we need if we are going to show compassion? We need *flexibility*. Part of the problem of those two who passed by on the other side was that they were very busy men. They had things to do, people to see, appointments to keep. More than that, they were religious men with very important responsibilities. They certainly would have liked to help the stranger, but there just wasn't time. Well, we don't know what kind of errand the Samaritan was on, but, as busy as he was, apparently his business could wait. How about us? Are we "interruptable?" Or is our daily schedule too tight for us to care? Does our plan for the day have any room in it for people along the way?

One more thing is noteworthy about that Samaritan. His compassion was *persistent*. He kept at it—medical attention, transportation, room and board, nursing care, and provision for the future. He really went overboard. That tests—and tests severely—the genuineness of any man's concern. It's easy to sympathize—even to the point of tears. It's easy, when moved by a generous impulse, to make a start at helping. But the follow-through is the tough part. Compassion that wears well—that's the real stuff.

Who is this Samaritan anyway? Is it I? Is it you? Is it anyone we know? There is one person, and only one, who fully fits the picture. And you know who that is. Jesus is the Good Samaritan to us all. He is the one who sees our need and can't forget it. He is the one who risks everything to do something for us. He is the one who can always be interrupted by any cry of human heartbreak. And he is the one who stands by us all the way through. Jesus loves us, finds us, saves us, even at the cost of his own life. And as he walks down that road toward Jerusalem we can hear him saying, "Come along behind me. Go and do likewise."

1. *Why does the exercise of compassion sometimes make people unpopular?*
2. *Do television programs depicting human need in various parts of the world help the viewers to care more? Why?*
3. *What do you think Jesus would have done if he had arrived on the scene while the robbers were still assaulting this traveler? Defend your answer.*
4. *We are all busy people. How can we fulfill our various responsibilities and still be responsive to emergency situations around us? Give examples.*
5. *Share instances you know of in which someone's compassion has been persistent over a long period of time. Why is this so hard for us?*
6. *What might Jesus' word "Go and do likewise" mean for you this week?*

11

A STRANGE COMBINATION

Background Scripture—Luke 10:38-42

> *Now as they went on their way, he entered a village; and a woman named Martha received him into her house. And she had a sister called Mary, who sat at the Lord's feet and listened to his teaching. But Martha was distracted with much serving; and she went to him and said, "Lord, do you not care that my sister has left me to serve alone? Tell her then to help me." But the Lord answered her, "Martha, Martha, you are anxious and troubled about many things; one thing is needful. Mary has chosen the good portion, which shall not be taken away from her"* (Luke 10:38-42).

Luke knew what he was doing when he put these two passages together—the parable of the Good Samaritan and the scene at the home of Mary and Martha. He holds up for us to admire and emulate, first, a man who shows compassion by the roadsides of life and then a woman who sits at Jesus' feet to hear his word. Now there's an unusual combination!

But not everyone thinks that these two are so praiseworthy. Not everyone approves of what they did. Remember the priest and the Levite who passed by on the other side? What would they have thought of the Samaritan's deed? We don't know, of course, but we know all too well how others of their countrymen usually felt about Samaritans. Maybe the priest and the Levite, when they read the tiny news items about it in the Jerusalem *Times,* reacted like this: "Did you read about what that Samaritan half-breed did out on the highway?"

"Yeah, one of those social-action do-gooders. The poor fish has no theology, no real heritage of faith. I guess this rescue act is his way of trying to work off his guilt and chalk up some points with God."

"Maybe so, but it won't help. If he doesn't belong to God's people, all his efforts are so much trash— 'filthy rags,' as the prophet put it. If there was any real godliness in that Samaritan and others like him, they would have come long ago to Jerusalem to offer true worship."

"You're right there. And I hear the man he brought into the hospital is, of all things, a Roman! Here these pagan Romans keep us down and drain us of everything we've got and along comes this Samaritan and keeps one of them alive. How unpatriotic can you get?"

So . . . not everybody likes the Good Samaritan. Many wonder if he is really so good after all. Nor do all approve of Mary, Martha's sister. Martha surely didn't. "Lord, don't you care that my sister has left me to serve alone? Tell her, then, to help me." Can't you hear her now? What she's really saying is this: "Lord, I'm of a practical sort; I like to get the job done. And look at Mary! She's sitting there doing nothing. I'm the real servant around here; I'm the one who ministers to the needs of others. And what does she do? Why, half the time she's in her prayer meetings and Bible studies. Lord, tell her to get where the action is, will you?"

It seems that the priest and the Levites—and the Marthas—are so hung up on their own specialty, and so blinded by a certain religious phoniness, that they can't recognize the real thing when they see it. But to Jesus, what the Good Samaritan did was beautiful. "Go and do likewise," he told the lawyer. And what Mary did was beautiful, too. "One thing is needful. Mary has chosen the good portion which shall not be taken away from her."

But how can you put these two things together? How can you possibly approve of both? They seem to express such radically different approaches to life. Yes, but look at Jesus Christ himself. He is a man among men, if there ever was one, pouring himself out in loving ministry to their needs. He is the man for others, living and dying for us. He is the Lord of Glory, stooping to serve. But that isn't all. Again and again he leaves the clamoring crowds, the pleas of pathetic folk waiting to be healed, and goes to some lonely place for communion with his Father. He seeks the Father's face, he waits for his direction, and he is refreshed in his presence. Jesus works *and* prays, listens *and* labors, receives from heaven *and* gives on earth. He puts it all together.

But what about us? Do we put it all together? Most of the time we don't. Whether we think of the church at large as polarized, or whether we are dealing with different groups in a single congregation, we tend to play off one emphasis against the other. We have people who are suspicious of what is called "social action," who are annoyed at certain efforts to relieve human suffering and need. They don't want to see time and energy and money put into controversial projects that offer little concrete return and that may involve cooperation with non-Christian agencies. And it's easy to find reasons which seem both orthodox and prudent to shoot holes in what the activists are doing.

But those activists, quite understandably, have a way of responding in kind. They sometimes have little interest in the devotional side of Christianity, in the disciplines of what is called "the spiritual life." They look on such concerns as senseless and irrelevant, totally unsuited for a world in revolution. And so they view the pietists among them with something of scorn, congratulating themselves all the while that they are men of action.

When will we get impatient with our little games? When will we stop splitting asunder what God has joined together? When will we learn to approve all that he approves? Oh, for that "strange combination"! God give us practical mystics, devoted reformers, complete Christians!

1. *In your better moments, whom are you most like—Mary or the Good Samaritan? Spell out the personality types represented in these two.*
2. *Of what traits in other Christians do you find yourself most critical? Why?*
3. *What are the strengths and weaknesses of what is called an "activistic" form of Christianity?*
4. *What are the strengths and weaknesses of what is called a "pietistic" form of Christianity?*
5. *How can we bring these two emphases together in a creative way? In what groups, ministries, or persons can you see this "strange combination?"*

12

HAPPINESS CAN'T BE "HAD"

Background Scripture—Luke 12:13-21

One of the multitude said to him, "Teacher, bid my brother divide the inheritance with me." But he said to him, "Man, who made me a judge or divider over you?" And he said to them, "Take heed, and beware of all covetousness; for a man's life does not consist in the abundance of his possessions." And he told them a parable, saying, "The land of a rich man brought forth plentifully; and he thought to himself, 'What shall I do, for I have nowhere to store my crops?' And he said, 'I will do this; I will pull down my barns, and build larger ones; and there I will store all my grain and my goods. And I will say to my soul, Soul, you have ample goods laid up for many years; take your ease, eat, drink, be merry.' But God said to him, 'Fool! This night your soul is required of you; and the things you have prepared, whose will they be?' So is he who lays up treasure for himself, and is not rich toward God" (Luke 12:13-21).

What a discouraging interruption! Jesus has been speaking to the multitudes about great things—the fear of God, the crucial importance of confessing the Son of Man, and the promised help of the Holy Spirit for every embattled witness. Suddenly one of his hearers breaks in with this rude request, "Teacher, bid my brother divide the inheritance with me" (v. 13). He is almost saying in effect, "I don't care about that other stuff you're telling us. What I want is someone to straighten out that grabby brother of mine!"

Isn't it remarkable what the prospect of an inheritance can do to people? It can poison the closest of relationships, sometimes setting brother against brother in lifelong enmity. And it can blind a person to what is really important in life. That is precisely what it did to this interrupter. Whatever Jesus had to say about the kingdom of God and the high destiny of men, this fellow had no ears to hear it. He was totally absorbed with that inheritance of which he felt himself cheated, and had no love any longer for the man he bitterly called "brother."

How can possessions do that to us? Why is it that a man will turn his back on God and rage against his closest relatives for the sake of an inheritance? "It's because he's covetous," we say. Yes, that is true; but what gives to covetousness its deadly power over us? The problem is that most of us seem to cherish the notion that possessions bring fulfillment, that wealth brings happiness. A man makes *having* the feverish quest of his whole existence because he believes that to have is to be, and to be rich is to be happy.

Jesus had little patience with this irritated demand. "Man, who made me a judge or divider over you?" (v. 14). If the complainer wanted someone to advance and defend his financial interests, he had come to the wrong person. Jesus didn't come for that. But this was only part of the delusion under which the man was laboring. Jesus attacks the deeper error when he says to all those around him, "Take heed, and beware of all covetousness; for a man's life does not consist in the abundance of his possessions" (v. 15). Apparently, we all need to watch out for this. It seems to be such a subtle snare that only constant vigilance can keep us from it. And if we are to have any defense against covetousness, we need to get one thing straight, says Jesus. "Possessions" do not equal "life." What a man has, can neither preserve his life nor fulfill it. I wonder if there is any teaching of our Lord's which is more cordially or widely disbelieved than that one! The proof of that is not hard to find. Wherever the desire to gain and to have becomes our absorbing interest in life, our unbelief is plainly showing.

Luke alone gives us the story that Jesus told to enforce this lesson. We call it "the parable of the rich fool." The rich man, it seems, has enjoyed an abundant harvest. Strangely, this increased wealth constitutes a problem for him. "What shall I do, for I have nowhere to store my crops?" (v. 17), he says. The more he gains, the more anxious he becomes about holding on to what he has. That hardly makes fortune-hunting the recipe for peace!

Now he has made his decision. "I will do this. I will pull down my barns and build larger ones; and there I will store all my grain and my goods" (v. 18). The possessive pronoun is so prominent here that it grates on the ear. To the rich man these are "my barns," "my grain," "my goods." His growing wealth blinds him to the most important fact about it, namely, its source. If the earth is the Lord's and the fullness thereof, if summer and harvest are his ordinances, and sunshine and rain his gifts, it is bad taste, to say the least, to forget him when we enjoy the fruits of the land. We are stewards. What we have, we have received from a fatherly hand and are accountable to him for what we do with it. This awareness, however, has faded completely from the rich man's mind.

But the man's last words really draw back the curtain and show us what lies deepest in his heart. "I will say to my soul, Soul, you have ample goods laid up for many years; take your ease, eat, drink, be merry" (v. 19). Here is the fatal error again—the idea that wealth guarantees happiness. The rich man congratulates himself—because he has so much, he will surely be secure for many years to come.

It is no wonder, in the light of this, that Paul can call covetousness *idolatry*. A man's possessions have become his idol, his little god, when he finds in them his security and expects from them his highest well-being. Whereas Christ says to men, "Come to me and I will give you *rest*," the man who surveys his riches says, "Take your *ease*." The word root is the same in each case. The covetous expect to receive from their possessions that which only their Maker and Lord can actually give.

That's what makes the rich man a fool. The fool lives his life as though God did not exist, as though anyone who has his assets in good order has no need of him. But the divine rebuke is, "Fool! This night your soul is required of you; and the things you have prepared, whose will they be?" Those riches, in other words, cannot prolong his life one hour, and he will derive little help from them when he dies. What folly, then, to set his hope upon them! And that folly, says Jesus, is shared by every person whose chief concern is to gather possessions for himself.

The alternative, of course, is to be rich toward God. "Seek his kingdom and these things shall be yours as well" (v. 31), Jesus says. Make God the

Lord of your life, his will the rule of your life, and his smile your hope of happiness. Then possessions will assume their rightful place. Love God, and use your gifts to express his love toward men. That's where life is to be found. Wealth and happiness really do go together, but not as the rich man thought they did. To make the Lord our treasure is to find in him our happiness, too.

1. What are the factors that make for tension within families over the matter of sharing an inheritance?
2. How does modern advertising try to convince us that life consists in what we possess? Give examples.
3. Does Jesus' answer in verse 14 imply that financial matters are unimportant to him? Discuss this.
4. What does this parable teach us about saving money for the future? What are the possible dangers in owning investments and securities?
5. How might we detect covetousness in our own lives? What practical measures can a Christian adopt to remain free of covetousness?
6. How would you describe what really makes for happiness? What place do possessions play in this picture?

13

THE GREAT REVERSAL

Background Scripture—Luke 14:7-11; 18:9-14

He also told this parable to some who trusted in themselves that they were righteous and despised others: "Two men went up into the temple to pray, one a Pharisee and the other a tax collector. The Pharisee stood and prayed thus with himself, 'God, I thank thee that I am not like other men, extortioners, unjust, adulterers, or even like this tax collector. I fast twice a week, I give tithes of all that I get.' But the tax collector, standing far off, would not even lift up his eyes to heaven, but beat his breast, saying, 'God, be merciful to me a sinner!' I tell you, this man went down to his house justified rather than the other; for every one who exalts himself will be humbled, but he who humbles himself will be exalted" (Luke 18:9-14).

God has a way of overturning the judgments of men. In the strange ways of his Kingdom, our modes of thinking are often contradicted. This is nowhere more clearly underlined than in Luke's Gospel. Luke records these words of Mary in which she sings of the God who reverses the fortunes of this world: "He has put down the mighty from their thrones and exalted those of low degree. He has filled the hungry with good things and the rich he has sent empty away" (1:52-53). Luke also quotes the saying of Jesus that those who hunger and weep now shall yet laugh and be satisfied, while those who now are full and merry will one day hunger and mourn. According to Jesus, God's evaluation of life in this world is strikingly different from ours. Indeed, "what is exalted among men is an abomination in the sight of God" (16:15). We men seem to go wrong most radically in the estimates we form of ourselves. It seems that however we look at ourselves, God turns the whole thing around. "For everyone who exalts himself will be humbled and he who humbles himself will be exalted" (14:11, 18:14).

As Luke records them, these words sum up the message of two parables which Jesus told. The first was about a marriage feast in which two patterns of behavior were illustrated. A man sat down in the place of honor and then was forced to take the lowest place because his host welcomed a more honorable guest than he. On the other hand, when a guest took the lowest place for himself, the host later escorted him to a place of greater honor.

The second parable is the well-known story of the Pharisee and the tax collector. Here was a Pharisee who prided himself on his virtues and thought that his relationship to God was secure. Jesus said, however, that the man was unacceptable. As for the tax collector, who called himself a sinner, Jesus seemed to contradict him, too. He said, "This man went down to his house justified." The Pharisee thought he was in the right but was really in the wrong. The tax collector knew he was in the wrong but then was declared to be in the right. What sense can we make of all this?

There is one thing we can quickly say that Jesus is *not* recommending here and that is a kind of false, tongue-in-cheek humility. That is to say, there is no meaning or merit in talking ourselves down for effect. We have all been wearied by people (and most of us have done some wearying, too) who advertise their failures and shortcomings at great length. The aim behind this, conscious or unconscious, is usually to have someone say, "Oh, no, you're not really that bad." It's a sort of sneaky, back-handed way to fish for compliments.

Nor does it mean low-rating your own gifts and accomplishments. There is nothing humble about announcing that you are a poor bowler when your average is in the 190s. Or in saying you have only an average voice when you can sing like Caruso. That kind of silly phoniness has given humility a bad name. How did we get the notion that in order to be humble you have to throw honesty out the window?

Often what passes for humility in a person is really a distorted self-image. Here is a young person who feels that he is no good, that he will never amount to anything, and that he will fail in everything he tries. Far from being a Christian virtue, that kind of self-depreciation and self-loathing is a tragically destructive influence in any human life. Such a person has never really heard what the Christian Gospel is saying at all. At least, he has never believed it for himself.

Well, what was wrong then about the guest who seated himself at the head table? Or the Pharisee who recited his virtues in the temple? Weren't they simply displaying a healthy self-concept? Why does God turn the tables on them? Part of the problem lies in the judgments that they were passing on others. To feel that you are a worthwhile person is a good thing. To feel that you are more worthy of honor and recognition than others is quite another matter. The first guest chose the superior place for himself, as though it were his due. The Pharisee showed the same tendency when he compared himself favorably with other men, considering himself to be out of their class. This is where pride comes in, especially when a man projects this kind of thinking heavenward and assumes that he is more deserving of God's favor and approval than other men. When we do this we are not only wronging our fellow-humans; we are also usurping God's place. Here is the worst error in our human pride. We assume that we are the ones who have the prerogative of passing judgment, whether on others or on ourselves. We act as if we knew the hearts of men, as if we could understand all the forces that play upon them, and weigh the motives for their actions. Worse still, we act as though we ourselves could speak the word that justifies, as though we sinful people could declare ourselves to be in the right with our Maker. This is the deadly evil, the sin that effectively damns us. For if we presume to justify ourselves, we can never hear the gracious divine word that does it for us.

What about the other guest? And what about the poor tax collector? There was nothing so great or virtuous about either one. Neither did anything that he could be particularly proud of. But this we can say for them: they didn't put themselves in a superior place. They didn't consider themselves as more worthy than others. And, most important, they left the matter of their acceptance, their exaltation, with God. They cast themselves on his mercy, without any presumption or claim, and waited for him to act. And in so doing, they acknowledged the truth of the Gospel that it is God who saves and not man.

Hear that strange word again. "Everyone who exalts himself will be humbled and he who humbles himself will be exalted." What is our Lord saying in this? He is saying, "Don't look down on other people as though you were more virtuous or valuable to God than they. And remember that it's always God who has the last word about you." In fact, God has already spoken that "last word" in his Son. The wonder of wonders is this: You don't have to make yourself acceptable or prove yourself worthy. In fact, when you say "no" to your pretensions and efforts to make it on your own, God says "yes" to you in Jesus Christ. That is the great reversal.

1. *What would be a good working definition of "humility"? Watch out for the stereotypes!*
2. *How would you distinguish between egotism and a "healthy self-concept"?*
3. *How is it possible to esteem others more highly than ourselves, especially when we seem to act in a more Christian way than they do?*
4. *What are the dangers involved in comparing ourselves with others?*
5. *Is it possible to be pharisaical about being like the publican—proud of being so penitent? Discuss this.*
6. *Can you think of other ways in which "the great reversal" applies?*

14

TOUGH TERMS

Background Scripture—Luke 14:25-33

Now great multitudes accompanied him; and he turned and said to them, "If any one comes to me and does not hate his own father and mother and wife and children and brothers and sisters, yes, and even his own life, he cannot be my disciple. Whoever does not bear his own cross and come after me, cannot be my disciple. For which of you, desiring to build a tower, does not first sit down and count the cost, whether he has enough to complete it? Otherwise, when he has laid a foundation, and is not able to finish, all who see it begin to mock him, saying, 'This man began to build, and was not able to finish.' Or what king, going to encounter another king in war, will not sit down first and take counsel whether he is able with. ten thousand to meet him who comes against him with twenty thousand? And if not, while the other is yet a great way off, he sends an embassy and asks terms of peace. So therefore, whoever of you does not renounce all that he has cannot be my disciple" (Luke 14:25-33).

It seemed as though Jesus' mission had now become a huge success. He was enjoying immense popularity. Luke tells us that as he made his way toward Jerusalem, "great multitudes accompanied him" (v. 25). The statistics of his growing movement would have impressed anyone.

Anyone, that is, except our Lord himself. Somehow large numbers of professed adherents failed to delight him. In fact, he was not nearly so skilled at holding together a vast following as many modern leaders are. He seemed bent on reducing their number. He made the demands of following him so stringent that he must have discouraged almost everyone.

Just think of how he treated these would-be followers! His first demand was, *no competition*. "If anyone comes to me and does not hate his father and mother and wife and children and brothers and sisters, yes, and even his own life he cannot be my disciple" (v. 26). This is a stern demand—and it sounds even sterner than it is. What? Hate your own loved ones? What kind of impossible requirement is this? Jesus was not saying, of course, that his followers are actually to hate one another, least of all their closest relatives. But he *is* speaking in the most emphatic way about what every disciple's foremost loyalty must be. These crises of conflicting attachments may not come along very often in life, but when they do, pleasing one's dearest loved ones must give way to pleasing the Lord.

The second condition for discipleship is equally drastic: *no self-preservation*. "Whoever does not bear his own cross and come after me cannot be my disciple" (v. 27). Our Lord had set his face to go to Jerusalem, and he knew that for him that meant a cross. Those who intended to follow him had to be prepared for the same thing. Sometimes we give this phrase, "bearing one's cross," a meaning that is foreign to Jesus' intention. Illness, handicaps, and difficult people may be hard to put up with, and may play a significant role in a Christian's sanctification, but they do not constitute a "cross." To the people of

Jesus' day the meaning of that term was inescapably plain. The cross was an instrument of torture and death. It was the form of execution most frequently used by the hated Romans. For a man to be seen bearing a cross meant one thing: He was on his way to die. Jesus was telling the multitudes, in other words, that if they meant to follow him they had to be ready to risk everything in the process.

Our Lord did not mean, obviously, that everyone who followed him would suffer crucifixion. But any prospective follower was to know that a readiness to die for Jesus' sake was required of him. Discipleship means loving Christ more than life itself.

What more could be demanded than this? Just when it seems that nothing further can possibly be said, Jesus concludes with a third requirement: *no exemptions*. In our internal revenue system there are certain parts of a family income for which the taxpayer may claim exemption. This means that a particular portion of his earnings is tax-free. The government has no claim on it. It belongs to the taxpayer, to use as he sees fit.

The claim of Jesus Christ, however, is a much more all-embracing one. "Whoever of you does not renounce all that he has cannot be my disciple" (v. 33). There is no possibility of exemption here. Everything a man has must be renounced if he intends to follow Christ. Once again, the requirement sounds strange to our ears. What can Jesus mean by that? Surely a man isn't expected to give away everything he has to the church or to the poor. What would he do then? No, it's not a matter of bankruptcy for every believer, but it does mean that a man adopts a particular attitude toward all that he possesses. He renounces all personal, exclusive rights to what he has. He acknowledges that he, together with all he possesses, is not his own but belongs to his faithful Savior Jesus Christ. He stands ready to use or part with anything and everything for the sake of that commitment.

What is Christ trying to accomplish by these absolute demands? Simply this: He wants those committing themselves to follow him to know exactly what they are getting into. He wants them to "count the cost." Does a man build a tower, he asks, without calculating the expense before he begins construction? Half a tower is a pretty ludicrous sight and will earn the embarrassed builder nothing but jeers. Or, asks Jesus, does a nation go to war without carefully assessing its chances of winning? If it appears that the odds are too great, it may be far wiser to sue for peace. It's a dangerous thing to start a fight that you can't finish. So, if a careful weighing of the prospects is important in any of our endeavors, how much more so in making life's supreme commitment?

How does all of this strike you? I must say that for me it is sometimes profoundly troubling. I have to ask myself, "Did I really count the cost when I made a commitment to Christ?" I'm afraid I didn't. I had only the faintest notion of what discipleship means. And even now, can I really say that I am ready to put Christ's claim ahead of the wishes of my loved ones? Am I prepared, if need be, to die for him or surrender all I have for his sake? I don't really know. All I can say is "Lord, I want to be your disciple. Whatever the cost is, this is the way I have chosen. But, Lord, how much I need your strength to work it out in daily living and how miserably I fail when I try to make it alone!" And then, one last question prods me. When I present Christ and the Christian life to others, am I fair and honest with them? Do I help them to count the cost in making a responsible decision, or am I so eager to make followers out of them that I hardly mention the cost at all?

1. What constitutes "success" for a church, or for an individual Christian?
2. What conflicts with loved ones may be involved in Christian discipleship? Give concrete examples.
3. What in your own experience most clearly illustrates what it means to "bear your cross?"
4. How would you recognize a person who had "renounced all that he had" to follow Christ?
5. How can we emphasize the conditions of discipleship without giving the impression that salvation is by works?
6. Are Christ's terms too "tough"? Express your feelings about this honestly.

15

HEAVEN'S JOY ON EARTH

Background Scripture—Luke 15:1-32

> *So he told them this parable: "What man of you, having a hundred sheep, if he has lost one of them, does not leave the ninety-nine in the wilderness, and go after the one which is lost, until he finds it? And when he has found it, he lays it on his shoulders, rejoicing. And when he comes home, he calls together his friends and his neighbors, saying to them, 'Rejoice with me, for I have found my sheep which was lost.' Even so, I tell you, there will be more joy in heaven over one sinner who repents than over ninety-nine righteous persons who need no repentance" (Luke 15:3-7).*

Huge neon letters spell out "JOY" atop the movie theatre at a busy downtown corner. On the marquee beneath them, the present and coming attractions are announced: "bawdy . . . uncensored . . . a real shocker. . . ." Apparently the joy that the proprietors have in mind is of a rather earthy sort.

You could write "JOY" in luminous letters over Luke's Gospel, too, but the joy of which he tells is different from the "X" grade movie variety. Luke tells about the joy of God's kingdom. No other Gospel writer sounds this note as strongly as he. As a famed New Testament scholar put it recently, Luke's writing is "dominated by future expectations and colored by ecstatic joy that the kingdom of God will come." Notice how this mood pervades his opening chapters. The birth of John the Baptist will bring joy and gladness to many, for he will prepare the way for the Lord's salvation (1:15). At the voice of Mary's greeting, the babe in Elizabeth's womb leaps for joy (1:44). Mary herself rejoices in God her Savior at the great things that he is about to do (1:47). And this joy, we quickly learn, is a "joy of heaven to earth come down." The tidings of great joy are brought by an angelic messenger: a Savior is born; salvation has come!

New joy bursts on men when they receive the promised salvation in Christ. Remember Zacchaeus? When Jesus called him to "make haste and come down," Zacchaeus did just that. He "made haste and came down and received Jesus joyfully." Receiving Jesus meant for Zacchaeus release from guilt and a new desire to share with others. He felt accepted in spite of what he had been before. To welcome such a Lord into our hearts and homes is to be, in C. S. Lewis' words, "surprised by joy."

And a Christian need not be apologetic because Christ has brought him joy. Some seem to view an emphasis on the joy of salvation as a bit superficial and irresponsible. "Aren't these people concerned about the needs around them, or aware of the tragic problems of our time?" But if believers, in spite of all this, keep on rejoicing in God's salvation, they need not fear. They have good warrant for that. When the disciples returned from a successful missionary enterprise, rejoicing at the fruit of their labors, Jesus expressly told them not to rejoice that the spirits were subject to them but rather to "rejoice that your names are written in heaven" (10:20).

Later on in the Book of Acts, Luke shows how the

Gospel brought joy wherever it went. When Philip came to Samaria preaching Christ, there was much joy in that city (Acts 8:8). The eunuch in the desert to whom Philip preached Jesus went on his way rejoicing after he had been baptized (Acts 8:39). And how glad the Gentiles were when they learned that the Gospel was for them (Acts 13:48)!

The good news of God makes men joyful because they learn in it that God cares for them, that in Christ he has done something wonderful on their behalf. They learn that in him they are cleansed from sin, released from bondage, and ushered into a new life. They become the children of God, assured of his unfailing love for them. And the future, therefore, is bright with hope. They rejoice, as Paul puts it, "in hope of sharing the glory of God."

In fact, this living hope of the Gospel makes it possible for Christians to rejoice in the most trying circumstances. The Lord himself commands them to do so. Listen to these astounding words: "Blessed are you when men hate you and when they exclude you and revile you and cast out your name as evil on account of the Son of Man. Rejoice in that day and leap for joy, for behold, your reward is great in heaven." Not only is it a joy to receive Christ; there is actually joy to be found in suffering for him. Joy in being hated, excluded, reviled, or rejected! Whatever is endured for the sake of Christ—because we belong to him and are identified with him—is cause for rejoicing. See how the early church found this to be true. Luke tells us that the apostles, after they had been beaten and forbidden to speak any more in the name of Jesus, "left the presence of the council, rejoicing that they were counted worthy to suffer dishonor for the name." Here it was—the very kind of rejoicing to which Jesus had called them. Paul and Barnabas had a similar experience. When storms of persecution drove them from one place to another, they "were filled with joy and with the Holy Spirit" (Acts 13:52).

Here was a new thing in the world. Joy and rejoicing were not, of course, unknown. And many before the days of the Christians had endured evils and persecutions with patient fortitude. But this joy in the midst of sufferings—that was something new. That people should not only endure the malice of others but actually be glad in the midst of it must have been baffling, almost overwhelming, to behold. This was the joy of God's kingdom breaking in upon a dreary earth.

But this joy of the kingdom of God, although it is intensely personal, is not a self-centered kind of gladness. It rejoices in the works of God, not only on behalf of ourselves but also as they affect others. When Jesus healed the sick on the Sabbath day, "the people rejoiced at all the glorious things that were done by him" (13:17). And the multitude of the disciples, when Jesus began his triumphal entry, "began to rejoice and praise God with a loud voice for all the mighty works that they had seen" (19:37). Christian joy is a joy in God and in the great things he has done for the children of men. In the life of Jesus himself, it was a joy in the Father's saving plan, whereby he hid his mysteries "from the wise and understanding and revealed them to babes" (Luke 10:21).

There is still a deeper sense, however, in which Christian joy is a joy "come down from heaven." In the fifteenth chapter of Luke are three parables in which joy plays a significant role. A shepherd finds his lost sheep and "lays it on his shoulders rejoicing" (15:5). A woman finds her lost coin and calls together her friends and neighbors saying, "Rejoice with me." And the father of a prodigal son calls all his household to eat and make merry, ". . . for this my son was dead and is alive again, he was lost and is found." In each of these unforgettable pictures, Jesus is illustrating the joy of heaven when one sinner repents and returns to God.

Here, perhaps, is the most telling test of our joy. To be happy in the blessings that we have received and yet unconcerned that others should share them is a strange perversion of joy. It surely cannot last, for no joy lives long without love. But when the things that make heaven rejoice make us joyful, too, we are surely on the right track.

1. What has been your greatest experience of joy? Share that with others.
2. How does Luke's view of joy differ from present-day popular conceptions?
3. Tell how you have seen the gospel of Christ bring joy to another person.
4. How is it possible to "rejoice" when you are being abused and injured? Does this involve suppressing or denying our natural human feelings?
5. Which is easier for you—to weep with those who weep, or to rejoice with those who rejoice? Can you tell why?
6. Does the idea that God "rejoices" over the repentance of sinners seem to make Him too "human"? Discuss this.
7. What connection do you see between love and joy?

16

THE LOVE THAT SEEKS

Background Scripture—Luke 15:1-32

*"And he arose and came to his father. But
while he was yet at a distance, his father saw
him and had compassion, and ran and em-
braced him and kissed him. And the son said
to him, 'Father, I have sinned against heaven
and before you; I am no longer worthy to be
called your son.' But the father said to his servants, 'Bring quickly the best robe, and put it
on him; and put a ring on his hand, and shoes
on his feet; and bring the fatted calf and kill it,
and let us eat and make merry; for this my son
was dead; and is alive again; he was lost, and is
found.' And they began to make merry" (Luke
15:20-24).*

What amazing balance there is in Luke's Gospel!
He has a genius for so bringing divergent emphases
together that his readers are never left with a one-
sided view of the truth. For example, if you were to
read Luke 14:25-35 all by itself you might gain the
impression that Jesus tried to discourage men from
following him. The demands of discipleship are made
so stringent and the cost so great that God seems
to be turning people away. But then along comes the
fifteenth chapter to round out the picture. Here God
is revealed as the one who seeks after those who wan-
der from him, and rejoices when they come back.

Luke 15 stands right at the heart of Luke's "travel
narrative," which is itself the center of his Gospel.

It includes three parables that appear in none of the other Gospels (although we hear of the ninety and nine and the one lost sheep in a slightly different context in Matthew). Each story has its distinctive message, but all share a common theme—the grandest theme of the Christian Gospel.

The setting for these parables is significant. Luke tells us that the tax collectors and sinners were all drawing near to hear him. Why did they come to him, these outcasts, these despised ones? Helmut Thielicke put it well: "An ineffable love radiated from him . . . and attracted from their usual haunts the very people whom nobody else cared for; people with loathsome, repulsive diseases, sinners who cowered before the contempt of society, the dejected and dismayed who normally concealed their misery from the eyes of others." That was it—an "ineffable love" shone out from him. But the Pharisees and scribes didn't see it that way. For them, his association with such people involved him in shame and guilt. They said, with indignation and contempt, "This man receives sinners and eats with them" (v. 2).

How right they were! Another sneering accusation had hit the mark earlier when they had called him a "friend of tax collectors and sinners" (7:34). Now in bitterness they spoke the sober truth again. Jesus did receive sinners. What his enemies hated in him, millions today love him for. He welcomes the unworthy. And here he told three parables to show that this very attitude that the Pharisees rejected is actually the outshining of God's glory. God's is a love that seeks after sinners.

In the first parable we see him as the shepherd who

goes out after his wandering sheep. In spite of all the hardship and suffering he may face, he is intent on bringing it back. Not even the presence of many others in the fold can content him as long as one of his own is lost.

Next, God is pictured as a woman searching for a lost coin. She lights a lamp; she sweeps the house; she carries on an intensive search until the missing coin is found. And how she rejoices when at last she finds it!

The third story is the fullest and richest of all. Now God appears as a father who deeply loves his sons. When one of them proves rebellious and wayward, the father watches for him in yearning love. When finally the boy remembers the father's house and turns penitently homeward, the father runs to meet him with arms outstretched, welcomes him back as a son, and rejoices over him with great joy. And when the other son, self-righteous and spiteful, refuses to join the festivities, the father goes out to meet him, too, longing for him to share the family's gladness.

If you are looking for something distinctive, something unique, in the Christian message, here it is. Judaism knew about God as the shepherd, but not as the seeker of lost sheep. Men had talked of him as "Father" before, but scarcely as one who pursues wastrels with his pardoning love. The Greeks would have considered this an unworthy trait in God. For them the ideal man did not know pity. God, then, being far greater, must be eternally unruffled and imperturbable. Islam knows no questing, suffering Lord, nor do the religions of the East. In Bangkok the immense figure of a recumbent Buddha expresses not an eager compassion, but rather a deliberate abstraction from the heartbreaks of life. In Jesus Christ alone, and supremely in his cross, does God appear in seeking, saving love.

But it is easy to admire the message of the parables —even to be moved by it—and still miss its application for us. Jesus told these stories not only to reveal what is in the Father's heart, but also to deal with what is all too often in ours. The Pharisees professed to know God and were for the most part serious about wanting to serve him. But they couldn't stand it when Jesus showed such interest in the "wrong" people. Well, who are the wrong people today? Who are the groups that many church folk regard with annoyance and hostility? Hippies? Demonstrators? Dope addicts? Black militants?

Now the situation becomes explosive. Suddenly the parables are not lovely little antiques; they are fighting words. How do we feel about people who associate with groups like those we have mentioned? What about those who spend their time in coffee houses with alienated youth, or in bars and taverns on "night ministry"? Is there something of disgust in our reaction? Of irritation? "But," we say, "they're not really bringing them the Gospel." That may be true in some cases, but even if it is, what then? Which is more Christian—to go among such and befriend them, or to stand aloof and criticize? "But," someone objects, "they don't deserve our help, and what's more, they don't even want it." Precisely what the Pharisees would have said about tax collectors and sinners. Or, "Why spend time and money on people like that?" Again, that's the echo of a question asked long ago. The more profound question for all who name Christ's name is this: Are we really happy with God's love—the way it *is,* not the way we imagine it to be? Do we find our hearts in tune with a shepherd scrambling after sheep that stray; or a father, with coattails flapping, running to meet his lost boy? If his love has really found us, we'll be joining in the search—and, oh, so glad when the lost are found!

1. *"This man receives sinners and eats with them." How do you reconcile this behavior of Jesus with the command quoted by Paul, "Come out from them, and be separate . . ." (II Cor. 6:17)?*
2. *What do you suppose were the qualities in Jesus that made him attractive to "publicans and sinners"?*
3. *What common features do you note in all three parables told in Luke 15?*
4. *In the light of these parables, how would you evaluate these comments by a church member: "The people in this community know that the church is here. If they want to come, they'll come. We don't need to call on them and invite them."*
5. *What kinds of "outsiders" or "different" people might not be welcome in your congregation?*
6. *How does the elder brother in the parable differ from his father? Which is your congregation most like? What about you?*
7. *A great theologian once said that the God of the Bible is "the God who comes." What did he mean by that?*

17

A WORD TO THE WEALTHY

Background Scripture—Luke 16:19-31

> *"But Abraham said, 'They have Moses and the prophets; let them hear them.' And he said, 'No, father Abraham; but if someone goes to them from the dead, they will repent.' He said to him, 'If they do not hear Moses and the prophets, neither will they be convinced if some one should rise from the dead'"* (Luke 16:29-31).

If you're not wealthy, you can skip this. It isn't meant for you. But wait a minute! Are you sure you're not rich? What of the billion-and-a-half people in the world who suffer from malnutrition—would you seem rich to them? You have more than enough food, haven't you? With a couple of changes of clothes and more than one pair of shoes, you would pass for a sultan in some cultures.

You say you have a car? A refrigerator? A TV set? Then you must be one of the rich ones after all. Millions of people in the world have little hope of ever owning any of these. I suppose you could say that any of us who have more than we need to stay alive and healthy are among the affluent. A rich man is any man who has something to spare—or share.

Jesus once told a very troubling story about wealth. Luke is the only one of the Gospel writers who has recorded it for us. It seems that a certain man was rich—that was about all you could say about him. He dressed himself in finery fit for a king and lived it up every day. Every meal was like a holiday banquet.

And then there was this other fellow named Lazarus. Just about all we learn of him is that he was poor. He was so poor that table scraps would have seemed like a feast to him. He was covered with sores, but the only medical attention he got was from a few mangy dogs. Lazarus used to lie at the rich man's gate. Can't you see him watching there with longing eyes as the guests went in and out and as the delivery boys came with each day's load of delicacies?

So far this story seems pretty familiar. We could find parallels to it almost anywhere today. Often the homes of the rich are very near the slums. And even if they aren't, there are more ways than ever before for the needy to peer in on the affluent. Most people take this situation more or less as a matter of course. That's the way it is. Some have it and some don't. It's great to be rich but bad news to be poor.

But now Jesus' story takes a new turn. Death comes, and everything has suddenly changed. Now we see the poor man carried by angels to Abraham's bosom, dwelling in heavenly bliss. The rich man, on the other hand, winds up in a place of torment. Around him is a flame that never goes out; and within, a thirst that can never be quenched. Now it is the rich man on the outside looking in, craving even the most paltry favor from the man who used to lie beyond his gate. "Father Abraham, have mercy upon me and send Lazarus to dip the end of his fingers in water and cool my tongue," he pleads. But his request is denied. His destiny is fixed, and no one can help him now.

What do you make of all this? Is Jesus teaching that the after-life simply reverses the fortunes of this life? Does he mean to make the rich tremble with apprehension while the poor rub their hands with glee? Does wealth turn out to be a crime and poverty a virtue? It may seem so at first glance, but that view of things leaves us with some real problems.

What about Abraham himself—the father of the faithful? Wasn't he a rich man? Surely wealth can't be evil in itself. Throughout the Bible it is viewed as a blessing from the Lord, not as a time-bomb to blast its owners into hell. And who, on the other side of things, would want to guarantee that a man who drinks or gambles himself into bankruptcy will prove a winner at the last? No, it's not that simple—either way.

The real key to the story is found in the last three verses, 29-31. When the rich man asks that Lazarus be sent to warn his brothers, Abraham says, "They have Moses and the prophets; let them hear them." And when the rich man further suggests that a messenger from the realm of the dead would be far more convincing, heaven's reply is, "If they do not hear Moses and the prophets, neither will they be convinced if someone should rise from the dead."

Apparently the crucial thing here is not whether we are rich or poor but how we respond to the Word of God. A man's eternal destiny is not settled by the size of his bank account but by what he does with the revelation of God. Apparently Lazarus has listened to the message of the Law and the Prophets. His trust was in the God of Abraham, Isaac, and

Jacob. His poverty, heartbreaking though it was, had not led him to bitter faithlessness. He was one of the *anawim,* the poor in spirit, to whom belongs the kingdom of God.

The rich man was different. He had never taken the Word of God seriously. He had never realized that both wealth and the power to acquire it are from the Lord. He had shut his ears against God's call to neighbor-love. He had turned his eyes away from the need and suffering at his own gate. Spurning the grace of God's Word, he had no heart to be gracious toward others.

Herein lies the searching message of the parable for us, the rich. We have more than the Law and the Prophets. We have the Gospels and the Epistles and the visions of the Apocalypse. We have heard God's last, best word in Jesus Christ. But have we truly responded to it? One of the tests is in how we view our wealth and what we do with it. If we can spend lavishly on ourselves and care nothing for human misery at our doorsteps, we are pagans still—whatever we may profess to believe. We are lost men and women —people without love, doomed to a loveless destiny. We may think we *have* a great deal, but in reality we have been *had*.

But if we listen—and keep on listening—to the word of God's salvation, our riches will never prove a snare to us. We who have freely received will freely give. We who have been shown compassion will be ready to show it. We who have known a great love will learn to love greatly. And no Lazarus at our door will look to us in vain.

1. On this 1 to 10 grid, including all the people in the world, where would you place yourself?

POVERTY 1 2 3 4 5 6 7 8 9 10 RICHES

2. Perhaps your financial situation has changed during the past few years. If it has, what effect do you feel this has had on your relationship to God?

3. Why do you suppose Jesus had so many sobering things to say about the use of wealth?

4. What are the various attitudes toward wealth held by Christians of your acquaintance? What biblical basis can you find for these attitudes?

5. Is tithing a responsible way of giving for all Christians? Explain your answer.

6. In what definite ways has your understanding of God's Word influenced your use of money?

18

ONLY THE GRATEFUL BELIEVE

Background Scripture—Luke 17:11-19

> *On the way to Jerusalem he was passing along between Samaria and Galilee. And as he entered a village, he was met by ten lepers, who stood at a distance and lifted up their voices and said, "Jesus, Master, have mercy on us." When he saw them he said to them, "Go and show yourselves to the priests." And as they went they were cleansed. Then one of them, when he saw that he was healed, turned back, praising God with a loud voice; and he fell on his face at Jesus' feet, giving him thanks. Now he was a Samaritan. Then said Jesus, "Were not ten cleansed? Where are the nine? Was no one found to return and give praise to God except this foreigner?" And he said to him, "Rise and go your way; your faith has made you well"* (Luke 17:11-19).

Think of all the people whom Jesus helped and healed during his public ministry. There must have been thousands of them. How many, do you suppose, expressed their thanks to him afterward? Here's a real shocker: As far as we know, there was only one! Only a Samaritan leper (whose name we don't even know) came back to say thanks.

There is something misleading about that way of putting it, of course. Doubtless many of those whom Jesus healed and saved were genuinely grateful and expressed that gratitude in word and life. But no express mention is made in the Gospels of their thankfulness. Only Luke, in telling us about the ten lepers whom Jesus met between Samaria and Galilee, tells us that someone gave thanks to Jesus Christ. And he calls special attention to this thankfulness because the other nine lepers apparently failed to show it.

Jesus was on his way to Jerusalem at the time. Since the Samaritans had refused to receive him (9:53), he was threading his way through the area where Samaria borders Galilee. As he entered a certain village, he was accosted by ten lepers. In keeping with the laws of the time, they kept their distance but apparently stationed themselves where he would have to notice them as he passed by. "Jesus, Master, have mercy on us!" they cried.

Jesus responded by telling them to go and show themselves to the priests. The lepers would have been familiar with this procedure. They knew that the Old Testament required of a person whose leprosy had been healed that he be examined by a priest. When the priest pronounced him cured, he could be readmitted to the normal life of the Jewish community. Jesus' command, in other words, implied a promise of healing. They were told to act as though their leprosy were already gone.

Upon hearing his word, the lepers left the scene. As they went to do what Jesus had told them, each was cleansed. What became of the other nine we do not know, but one came back. Praising God at the top of his lungs, he prostrated himself before Jesus and gave thanks. To him Jesus said, "Rise and go your way, your faith has made you well."

Now why did Luke include this striking little narrative in his Gospel? Did he want to show that true gratitude is a rare thing? Was he trying to emphasize that despised Samaritans are sometimes more responsive to God's grace than the Jews who despise them? Perhaps both of those things were in his mind. Both certainly bear pondering. But there is something more here that needs careful attention. The account of the ten lepers shows us *the link between thankfulness and faith*.

In one sense, all of these afflicted men demonstrated faith in Jesus. All called upon him for mercy —that is certainly an act of faith. They would not have appealed to him for aid without some glimmer of hope that he would help them. And certainly they showed faith when they obeyed Jesus' word and started off to see their priests. With nothing to go on except his word, they trusted him enough to venture on it. And they found healing. So far, so good. You can't ask much more than that, can you?

But Jesus wasn't satisfied. He wanted more than that from these men. There was something of pain and disappointment in the question he asked: "Were not ten cleansed? Where are the nine? Was no one found to return and give praise to God except this foreigner?" It seems that only the Samaritan had demonstrated the faith which Jesus longed to see.

This thankful ex-leper had realized, for one thing, who Jesus was. When he fell at Jesus' feet, praising God, he was making the right connection. He knew that Christ had done for him what only God could do. Or, to put it another way, he knew that God had touched him in the person of Jesus Christ. We don't know how the others felt about Jesus. Perhaps to them he was only the means to a desired end. He was someone who had the power to heal them, but beyond that they didn't care very much who he was. They never saw beyond the gift to the giver.

There's something special about a faith that gives thanks. Our Samaritan came near to Christ, nearer than he had ever been before. The faith that remembers him with gratitude brings us into vital personal touch with the Savior. Faith, in the full-orbed New Testament sense, is not merely a conviction that Jesus can do something for us. It is also a new relationship to God through him. And if there is something greater than healing, it is to know the healer. Salvation itself would be a strange and hollow thing if it did not bring us to the Savior himself.

What's the message of all this for us who call ourselves the people of God in the twentieth century? May it not be this: "Examine yourselves, prove your own selves whether you be in the faith"? The fact that you pray is right and good, but it does not guarantee a living faith. Your acting upon his promise is a grand thing, too. But even though you've done this and have experienced something of his transforming power in your life, that's not the end of the matter. He looks for a faith in you which sees the gracious intention behind his gifts, that acknowledges the undeserved love incarnate in him, and that returns to him again and again with the offering of praise and thanks. This is the sign that we have received the best gift. To all such cleansed ones Jesus says, "Your faith has made you well."

1. In what sense is thankfulness a sign of true faith?
2. Why does it mean so much to us when people appreciate what we do for them?

3. What are some of the services you have rendered recently for which no one has thanked you?
4. What kindnesses have been done to you in the last few days for which you haven't yet given thanks?
5. We often think of a regular devotional life as providing us with strength and renewal for Christian living. In the light of this passage, what would you say that our daily devotions mean to God?
6. At what times in your life have you felt most grateful to God? What should we do about thanksgiving when we don't feel grateful?

19

PRAYER AND DISCOURAGEMENT

Background Scripture—Luke 11:1-13; 18:1-8

> *And he told them a parable, to the effect that
> they ought always to pray and not lose heart.
> He said, "In a certain city there was a judge
> who neither feared God nor regarded man;
> and there was a widow in that city who kept
> coming to him and saying, 'Vindicate me
> against my adversary.' For a while he refused;
> but afterward he said to himself, 'Though I
> neither fear God nor regard man, yet because
> this widow bothers me, I will vindicate her, or
> she will wear me out by her continual coming.'"
> And the Lord said, "Hear what the unrighteous
> judge says. And will not God vindicate his
> elect who cry out to him day and night? Will
> he delay long over them? I tell you, he will
> vindicate them speedily. Nevertheless, when
> the Son of man comes, will he find faith on
> earth?" (Luke 18:1-8).*

"Don't talk to me about prayer! I've tried it and it
doesn't help." Some of us, perhaps, would not voice
the complaint quite so boldly, but what Christian
hasn't known something of the discouragement that
lies behind that outburst? We pray, yes, but illnesses
wear on and burdens grow no lighter. We plead for
others before God, but their situation doesn't change.
We intercede for the work of Christ's kingdom, but
the forces of evil in the world still seem secure and
strong. Secret doubts begin to gnaw at the vitals of
our faith: "Does praying really make any difference?"

Luke seems to have been especially sensitive to this struggle in the Christian life. In the lengthy section on following Jesus "in the way," he includes two parables that speak directly to the problem of discouragement. Neither parable appears anywhere else in the New Testament, so here again we are indebted to Luke for a distinctive emphasis.

In the first story, Jesus sketches a delightful little scene from life. It is late at night. A man has received an unexpected visitor and has nothing in the house with which to feed him. An earnest hospitality drives him out into the street—even in the black of night—to seek bread from a friend. He knocks and makes request, only to receive a gruff and sleepy refusal. Unabashed, he knocks more loudly. By this time, all the dogs in the neighborhood are barking. Here and there along the street an angry voice is heard, and a tousled head pops into view. Swallowing his embarrassment, our seeker knocks on. Finally there is action. The friend within can take it no longer. In quiet desperation, he throws open the door and gives the shameless visitor all the bread he needs.

The second parable centers on another request, though in a quite different setting. Here the suppliant is a widow who has been gravely wronged. She makes her appeal to a judge who is completely without principle. He has no sense of responsibility toward God nor the slightest regard for the rights of others. It hardly seems like a promising situation for an appeal. But she keeps coming with her request until finally the judge decides to do something for her—if only to gain a moment's peace.

What is Jesus teaching us in these unforgettable vignettes? For one thing, he makes it plain that prayer is *meant to be answered*. Now that may seem like belaboring the obvious, but there is need for it. The idea has become current among many people that the value of prayer ends with the effect it has upon the person who prays. Praying is viewed as a psychological exercise that is somehow "good for us," but that is about all. But the God of whom Jesus speaks is the living God, the God who hears. The Christian who truly prays is not talking himself into something. Prayer is more than autosuggestion. Didn't our Lord teach with unwearied repetition that true prayer will be answered? He makes that point no less than six times in the space of two verses (11:9-10). And each parable ends with the petitioner receiving the very boon he sought.

But how are we to understand these two grudging givers? Is Jesus saying that God is like that—a grouchy sleeper? A heartless judge? No, the force of the argument depends on the happy truth that God is *not* like that. Jesus is arguing from the less to the greater, from the worse to the better. If even the drowsy and reluctant can be prevailed on to help, how much more God? If a judge without conviction or compassion will yield to the quest of a stranger, what will the gracious and faithful God be willing to do for his children? Jesus brings it even closer to our experience when he asks, "If you, then, who are evil, know how to give good gifts to your children, how much more will the heavenly Father give the Holy Spirit to those who ask him?" (11:13).

But these assurances about God's faithfulness in answering prayer are written large in all the Gospels—throughout the Bible, for that matter. The special stress in each of these parables is on the *per-*

sistence of those who make the requests. The man at the door keeps on knocking; he will not go away. The widow before the judge keeps on pleading; she refuses to be silenced. And here is where the tie-in comes with our problem of discouragement. Jesus told his disciples the second of these parables "to the effect that they ought always to pray and not to lose heart" (18:1). He knows how prone we are to "lose heart." And so he etches these vivid pictures deeply into our minds, that we may know that our labor of prayer will not be in vain. The alternative to discouragement is to keep on praying—with our eyes upon the faithful, giving God.

Some people have a problem with this idea of persistence, of importunity. To them it seems almost an act of unbelief. If we have sincerely prayed to the God who answers prayer, what point is there in repeating the request? Doesn't that show that we doubt? Doesn't that imply presumption on our part, as though we were trying to persuade an unwilling God?

But, plausible as these arguments seem, persistence and faith are friends, not enemies. We persist not because we doubt but because we desire so much the promised blessing. And faith seems to grow strongest and purest in the discipline of delay. So whether you pray for the progress of the Gospel, or intercede with a burdened heart for others, or cry to God for the deepest needs in your own life, remember the widow and the friend at midnight. Pray, and don't lose heart. Or better, pray and you *won't* lose heart!

1. *What experiences in your life have most encouraged you in the faith that God answers prayer?*

What situations have most threatened to discourage you?

2. *Why would you say that the widow and the midnight seeker were so persistent? Should these motivations be present in the prayers of Christians? Discuss this.*

3. *What is the difference between genuine importunity in prayer and what Jesus called "vain repetitions" (Matt. 6:7)?*

4. *Why do you suppose God wants his people to "keep on asking" in their prayers? Doesn't he know what we want? Isn't one request sufficient?*

5. *What is the relationship between God's promises and our prayers? Can we be more certain that some prayers will be answered than others?*

20

PREVENTIVE PRAYER

Background Scripture—Luke 21:34-36;
22:39-46

> *And he came out, and went, as was his cus-*
> *tom, to the Mount of Olives; and the disciples*
> *followed him. And when he came to the place*
> *he said to them, "Pray that you may not enter*
> *into temptation." And he withdrew from them*
> *about a stone's throw, and knelt down and*
> *prayed, "Father, if thou art willing, remove this*
> *cup from me; nevertheless not my will, but*
> *thine, be done." And there appeared to him*
> *an angel from heaven, strengthening him. And*
> *being in an agony he prayed more earnestly;*
> *and his sweat became like great drops of blood*
> *falling down upon the ground. And when he*
> *rose from prayer, he came to the disciples and*
> *found them sleeping for sorrow, and he said to*
> *them, "Why do you sleep? Rise and pray that*
> *you may not enter into temptation"(Luke 22:39-*
> *46).*

Christ lifts up the fallen and restores those who
fail. That is the Gospel truth. But we can pervert its
truth by the use we make of it. What is meant as a
comfort for the penitent can become a pillow for the
complacent. Instead of hope for those who weep over
their sins, it becomes an excuse for those who make
light of them. This is the final perversion of his grace:
"Let us do evil that good may come. Let us fall that
he may pick us up."

Nothing in the Gospel was ever meant to teach
that. Whoever makes defeat the norm and sets a

premium on failure has twisted the good news. Christ brings deliverance as well as pardon. The one who lifts the fallen can also keep them from falling again. Peter's denial has a message of hope and encouragement for us, not only because he was restored but because thereafter he was faithful unto death.

Our Lord, as he is presented in Luke's Gospel, warns his disciples repeatedly about the pitfalls before them. They will be under constant pressure to go back on their discipleship, to deny their Lord. Failure, even total failure, will be an ever-present possibility for them. Their hearts may become heavy and dull, either by thanklessly enjoying the things of earth or by worrying about the lack of them. The purposes of God's kingdom and the hope of the Lord's appearing may thereby become remote and unreal to them. Even while professing their Lord, they may live as those who are shamefully unprepared for his coming.

What a gloomy prospect! Can this be what we were redeemed for? Is there nothing more to the Christian life than this? God forbid! These words of Christ are a warning, not a prophecy. He tells us of this grim possibility so that he may fortify us against it. What, then, must we do? His word is, "Watch at all times, praying that you may have strength to escape all these things that will take place and to stand before the Son of Man." Since we are weak, and since the pressures against us are so subtle and strong, we are called to constant vigilance together with prayer. Prayer is especially recommended as a means of securing strength—strength to avoid all these perils to the life of faith.

In Luke's next chapter the need for this is vividly illustrated. Before our Lord withdrew from his disciples to give himself to prayer, he urged them, "Pray that you may not enter into temptation." Like the last petition in the Lord's Prayer, this is a plea that we may not *yield* to temptation. It is a prayer that God will not withdraw his hand from us, leaving us helpless before the powers of evil. Jesus knew that grim testing was ahead for his disciples and he urged them to prepare for it by prayer—"preventive prayer." Later, after his own praying was completed, he repeated the charge, "Rise and pray, that you may not enter into temptation." The implication of this charge is plain. Our Lord was convinced that if his disciples did not pray they would succumb to the power of temptation.

Apparently this was difficult for the disciples to believe. Peter, for example, was sure that he would never fail Christ. "Lord, I am ready to go with you to prison and to death," he protested. It seemed inconceivable to him that he would ever deny his Lord. In spite of Jesus' repeated command and warning, Peter and others did not keep up their vigil in Gethsemane. They were drowsy and depressed. What little urgency they felt for prayer was soon overcome. They fell asleep. Then came the hour of Jesus' enemies, "the power of darkness," and not a man of those disciples was able to stand by his Lord. They didn't have what it took.

Our problem is much the same. Like Peter, we are sure about our sincerity as Christ's followers. We have no intention of deserting or denying him— that would be the farthest thing from our minds. But we trust far too much in our own steadfastness. Even when others whose faith we have admired make shipwreck in their Christian course, we rarely take it to heart. In fact, we may have a sense of smugness about it all. "So and so turned out to be a pretty weak Christian." We, of course, have far more stability than that!

And how we underestimate the deadly strength of temptation! Our Lord's sober, repeated warnings seem to us like "much ado about nothing." When the apostle Peter talks about the devil going about as a "roaring lion seeking whom he may devour," we take it as a rather exaggerated metaphor. But Peter would not have agreed—not after that night in the high priest's court. For him the craft, the malice, and the power of the tempter had become so real that no less vivid figure would suffice—a ravaging lion.

"But," says someone, "that still sounds grossly overdrawn. I've scarcely had time to pray for weeks, and yet you don't find me denying Christ or wallowing in wickedness." Perhaps not. But that doesn't make our Lord's warning any less true or needful. Maybe our Christian life and witness are so anemic already that we scarcely need tempting. Or maybe the moment of severe testing has yet to arrive. But if our Lord is any authority on the realities of the Christian conflict, this much at least is certain: No man is strong enough to resist and overcome evil without divine strength. And no man can live long in that strength without preventive prayer.

1. Why are Christians, even though redeemed by Christ and indwelt by God's Spirit, still susceptible to temptation and spiritual decline?
2. How does prayer strengthen us against temptation?

3. Why was Peter confident that he would not deny Christ?

4. What is the difference between Christian watchfulness and a nervous "walking on eggs"?

5. Discuss this strong statement by the English theologian, P. T. Forsyth: "The worst sin is prayerlessness. Overt sin, or crime, or the glaring inconsistencies which often surprise us are the effect of this, or its punishment. We are left by God for lack of seeking Him" (P. T. Forsyth, The Soul of Prayer, p. 11).

6. What experiences of failure have you known in your Christian life? What steps can you take to avoid a recurrence?

21

CHRIST AND OUR FAILURES

Background Scripture—Luke 22:28-34, 54-62; 24:34

"Simon, Simon, behold Satan demanded to have you, that he might sift you like wheat, but I have prayed for you that your faith may not fail; and when you have turned again, strengthen your brethren." And he said to him, "Lord, I am ready to go with you to prison and to death." He said, "I tell you, Peter, the cock will not crow this day, until you three times deny that you know me" (Luke 22:31-34).

Where is Christ when we really make a mess of things? We can see his hand in our successes (at least we ought to), but what about in our failures? Have we a theology for defeats?

Perhaps the classic instance of Christian stumbling is Simon Peter's denial. At least it is the most widely publicized! All four Gospels include the dismal account: Peter professing his deathless loyalty, Jesus predicting his denial, and then Peter wilting before his questioners. What a book of truth the Bible is! Even its most notable men of faith appear "warts and all." All the world knows how shamefully the great apostle failed his Lord.

Luke, however, throws more light on this happening than anyone else. He includes additional scenes before, during, and after the event, which greatly enrich its meaning for us. Most significantly, they reveal the ministry of Christ amid the failures of his people.

First, there is Christ's prayer for Peter: "I have prayed for you that your faith may not fail." Our Lord draws back the curtain here on what transpires behind the scenes of our earthly life. In a passage reminiscent of the Book of Job, he speaks of the tempter's designs against Peter. "Simon, Simon, behold Satan demanded to have you that he might sift you like wheat." The devil seeks to bring about Peter's fall. He wants to bring Peter into a testing that will prove the disciple false. Satan would like to see the wheat disappear and only the chaff remain. His is a sifting of malice; his end is Peter's destruction. But, says Jesus, "I have prayed for you." This, he seems to say, is Peter's sole defense against the tempter's scheme. Apart from this, the "sifting" would have been successful. Peter would never have recovered from its effects. But the intercession of Jesus is mighty to help. Although Peter fails miserably, his faith does not fail.

This is one of the few passages in which Jesus speaks in a specific way about his own prayers. What does he pray for, and what does this intercession actually accomplish? Apparently he prays for his people, that they may be preserved in faith. He does not pray that they may be kept from stern testings or even from humiliating failures, but he pleads with mighty efficacy that even in the midst of struggles and shameful inconsistencies they will not finally fall away. Though Peter loses his way for a time, he will turn back. Jesus says, *"When* you have turned again" —not *if* you do.

Now we are in the courtyard of the high priest's

house. Peter, when pressed to admit that he is one of Jesus' followers, denies with a curse that he even knows him. The words of his denial are no sooner out of his lips than there comes the sound of the cock crow. Here Luke adds a significant touch which is found in none of the other Gospels: "And the Lord turned and looked at Peter." Perhaps Jesus was being led from one room to the next in the course of his trial. Perhaps the room in which he was being held opened out onto the court. What the exact circumstances were and what that look was intended to convey, we can only surmise. But Luke seems to suggest that Christ's look awakened Peter's conscience. He "remembered the word of the Lord and he went out and wept bitterly."

Where is Christ in the failures of his people? He is there, precisely when they fail. He sees our treachery; he hears our denial; he knows our shame; and in the midst of it he looks upon us with a look that neither condemns nor excuses. But it does break our hearts and lead us to repentance. This is his saving mercy. Jesus comes to us in the very moment of our fall and begins to turn our hearts back again.

Luke adds one more touch to make the picture complete. On Easter evening, when the gathered disciples meet the men from Emmaus, they exclaim, "The Lord has risen indeed and has appeared to Simon!" Apparently (and this is borne out in I Corinthians 15:5) there was a special appearance of the risen Lord to Simon Peter. Again, we don't know exactly what took place in that meeting. We can only marvel that Christ chose to manifest himself first to the man who had so blatantly denied him. We do know, however, that this encounter with the resurrected Christ was the turning point in Peter's career. He did "turn again." He did realize the promise of his name, becoming a rock-like apostle. And, as his Lord commanded him, he was able from that time forward to "strengthen his brethren" (read I Peter, for example).

Now we can see the whole picture. In all our experience of failure and defeat, Christ is at work. Seeing our weakness and peril, he prays that we may be sustained. He comes to us in our worst hours and leads us to a godly grieving. When we scarcely dare to believe that we can serve him again, he meets us with incredible mercy to give us a fresh start. And through all of this, he makes us able to encourage and support our struggling brethren. He is the Savior of those who sin, the help of all who fail.

1. How can even our failures serve to promote our growth in Christ?
2. Why do you suppose the record of Peter's denial is given such prominence in the Gospels?
3. How is Peter's experience similar to that of Job? How different?
4. The New Testament teaches that Christ is interceding for us now. What evidence does it provide as the content of his prayers on our behalf?
5. When the Lord "looked at Peter" (Luke 22:61), what do you feel was communicated in that look?
6. How did this whole experience equip Peter to "strengthen his brethren"? What helps you most— when others share their victories, or when they tell of their failures and struggles?
7. How have you experienced Christ's presence and work in the midst of failure?

22

SAVE YOURSELF!

Background Scripture—Luke 23:32-43

And the people stood by, watching; but the rulers scoffed at him, saying, "He saved others; let him save himself, if he is the Christ of God, his Chosen One!" The soldiers also mocked him, coming up and offering him vinegar, and saying, "If you are the King of the Jews, save yourself!" There was also an inscription over him, "This is the King of the Jews."

One of the criminals who were hanged railed at him, saying, "Are you not the Christ? Save yourself and us!" (Luke 23:35-39).

Why not save yourself? That was the great temptation. Our Lord wrestled with it first in the wilderness. "If you are the Son of God, command this stone to become bread" (Luke 4:3). "After all," the tempter reasons, "a man has to live. How long are you going to wait for God to provide? You can do it on your own. Save yourself!"

Jesus heard it again in the clamor of the crowd for a sign, and in their whispered plans to make him a king. He heard it even in the sugary words of a well-meaning friend. "God forbid, Lord, this shall never happen to you" (Matt. 16:22). "All this about suffering, rejection, and death at Jerusalem—that's not for you." But with lightning in his eyes he rebuked Peter. "Get behind me, Satan." In that affectionate remonstrance he heard the same siren song, "Save yourself."

But the final struggle came on Golgotha. The taunts seemed to come from everywhere. Luke records three successive incidents in which the pressure mounted. First there were the politicians jeering at him beneath the cross. "He saved others; let him save himself if he is the Christ of God, his chosen one!" (23:35). And the soldiers, mockingly, as they offered him vinegar, said, "If you are the king of the Jews, save yourself!" (23:37). Even from one of the dying men beside him came words like these, loaded with venom and scorn; "Are you not the Christ? Save yourself and us" (23:39). Save yourself! Save yourself! Save yourself! In a kind of fiendish chorus, he was tempted to the very last.

And isn't this the snare which his servants face, too? Many and subtle are the forms it takes. There is the pressure to save ourselves from *blame*. Like Adam or Aaron or Saul, we find it seductively easy to shift responsibility. And so we save our own reputation by sacrificing someone else's. Another is condemned so that we may go free. Or perhaps it's to save ourselves from *ridicule*. When truth is unpopular and when the right thing is not the "in" thing, how easy it is to hedge a bit or at least to keep quiet. After all, no one wants to make a fool of himself! Or maybe our self-saving is along another line. We spare ourselves *inconvenience*. When a wife or husband needs to talk, when children hunger for attention, or when friends drain us with their troubles, we pull back. How hard it is to put yourself out! How much more natural to spare yourself a little.

A congregation can do this. "We'd like to reach out to our community, but what would happen to our church if some 'undesirables' started to attend here?"

Or a whole denomination can do it. We have heard interesting arguments on both sides of the various merger issues. Instead of weighing the comparative possibilities for ministry, we too often ask questions like this: "What will become of our church if we go into this merger?" Or, "What will become of us if we try to struggle on alone?" And how often has the church in its wider dimensions also seemed to lose its life while struggling to save it?

Some of us, it is true, have become experts at losing our lives. We have made that a new orthodoxy. It's possible to glory in blame and ridicule, to see it as the height of achievement if we can get ourselves ejected or jailed. But when we choose the scene of our own martyrdom and manage to have the right people watching, it may not be a losing of our lives at all, but just another bid to enhance the old ego. There is more than one way to save yourself.

No, it's all in the motivation behind it. Our Lord refused to save himself, but it was not because he lacked the power—certainly not because he hated life! And he wasn't out to impress anyone. His aim was to save *us*. They mocked him, saying, "He saved others; let him save himself." It seemed reasonable to them that if he had done it for others he should be able to do it for himself. But that was precisely what he could not do. His words, "Father, forgive them" and "Today you shall be with me in paradise" pointed to the purpose of his entire ministry. We are the guilty ones who needed saving. Instead of sparing himself, he chose to save us. And that cost him his life.

For us, too, there is no value in sacrifice *per se,* no glory in suicide. Why then should the church risk anything? Why stand against the subtle temptation to save ourselves? "For my sake and the gospel's," says Jesus. Because we love him and those for whom he died—that's why. That makes sacrifice glorious, and the losing of ourselves, eternal life.

1. What common thread can you see running through all three of Jesus' temptations in the wilderness?
2. How is the church in your community most tempted to "save" itself? What are your greatest personal temptations to "save" yourself?
3. Is our "instinct of self-preservation" a good thing? If so, how does a healthy self-preservation differ from "saving" ourselves?
4. Does self-denial involve having a low opinion of yourself? Explain.
5. What contemporary examples can you cite of Christians "losing their lives" for Christ's sake and the gospel's?
6. In what areas of your life as a church and as an individual do you believe that Christ is calling you to take risks?

23

THE SAVIOR AND THE SINNER

Background Scripture—Luke 23:39-43

> One of the criminals who were hanged railed
> at him, saying, "Are you not the Christ? Save
> yourself and us!" But the other rebuked him,
> saying, "Do you not fear God, since you are
> under the same sentence of condemnation? And
> we indeed justly; for we are receiving the due
> reward of our deeds; but this man has done
> nothing wrong." And he said, "Jesus, remem-
> ber me when you come in your kingly power."
> And he said to him, "Truly, I say to you, today
> you will be with me in Paradise" (Luke 23:39-
> 43).

Though tempted to the end to save himself, Jesus
was intent on saving us. This was the heart of his mission. "The Son of man came," he said, "to seek and
to save the lost" (19:10). Not even mortal agony
could deflect him from that aim. In dying as in living,
he was above all else the *Savior*.

Luke sounds this note more than any of the other
Gospel writers. If for Matthew Jesus is chiefly the
promised King, for Mark the mighty Son of Man, and
for John the Son of the living God, he is for Luke the
gracious Savior. The words "savior" and "salvation"
appear more often in his Gospel than in the other
three combined. But there is more to it than words.
Luke is especially concerned to show us Jesus in saving *action*.

You remember the scene. All around the Crucified

116

swirls a tempest of hate and reviling. Priests wag their heads in scorn. Soldiers toss up their coarse jests. Even the thieves on either side of him jeer bitterly. How strange, how foreign to the scene, is his first word, "Father, forgive them for they know not what they do!" One thief grows suddenly silent. He seems profoundly affected by what he has just heard. Who wouldn't be?

But the man on the other side of the cross is unimpressed. Again he challenges the sufferer beside him. "Are you not the Christ? Save yourself and us!" (v. 39). This time an answer comes back quickly, not from the center cross but from beyond it. For the first and only time a man on Golgotha speaks in Jesus' defense. Who would have expected it from a condemned criminal? What had happened to this other thief?

Here is *repentance*—the thing itself happening before our eyes. The man's whole outlook is changed. Until this time he has known the law of the land, known that his deeds are evil, known that he might be caught and punished. In that sense he has realized his wrongdoing all along, but perhaps like that raging man on the other cross he has never really faced what he is. He has never admitted to himself and to others his guilt, his ill deserving. Now it seems that he sees in the One beside him the man he should have been, and that breaks him down. "We are receiving the due reward of our deeds, but this man has done nothing wrong" (v. 41). There is something about the suffering of the innocent that awes and shatters us.

But the thief saw more than that—more than a blameless sufferer. In the One beside him he glimpsed the pardoning love of God toward the guilty. He heard God's whisper in the words, "Father, forgive them." And that's what leads us to true penitence—the sight of our guilt and ugliness against the background of his suffering love.

Real repentance, then, is never far away from *faith*. We only turn from our sins when we find a gracious God to turn to. We have no heart to repent until his mercy dawns upon us. And how it dawned upon this man! Unbelief was all around him. Most of the onlookers had never trusted Jesus. Those who had, had almost lost hope. Others were shouting, "If you are the King of the Jews," do this or that.

But for this convict there were no "if's." "Jesus, remember me when you come in your kingly power" (v. 42). The thief was no theologian, of course. He understood precious little of the real significance of Jesus' death. And yet that simple prayer of his was throbbing with genuine faith. For one thing, he saw and believed that Christ was a king. He believed also this incredible thing, that the One dying in weakness beside him would come one day with royal power. And more than that, he called on Jesus as one who could help him even on the other side of death.

There is a touching, refreshing simplicity about this kind of faith. How it sweeps away a host of non-essentials! How it exposes our cluttered notions of what it is to believe! Can baptism be essential for salvation? Surely it was not for this man. Are good works required, then, for acceptance? This man had none and no time left to perform any. What about membership in a religious institution? He wouldn't have had the faintest notion of what that means.

Had he lived longer, had he survived the ordeal of the cross, things would probably have been different.

Surely then he would have been baptized, would have joined himself to his fellow Christians, would have adorned his faith with good works. But the fact is that he didn't. It's the thing he *did* do that is so significant. He called upon Jesus out of a penitent heart. That is the faith of the Gospel—simple and grand.

But this prayer of the dying penitent, beautiful as it is, is not the best thing that happened there in those last moments. The good news is not in his plea but in Jesus' promise. "Truly, I say to you, today you will be with me in Paradise" (v. 43). He gave that seeker far more than he asked. The man prayed, "When you come," but Jesus promised, "Today." He asked wistfully, "Remember me—give a thought to the one who suffered with you," but Jesus pledged him, "You will be with me."

Here again, if anything can clear away the mists that obscure what *salvation* means, it is this scene. If ever a man deserved to be lost, it was this self-confessed criminal. If anyone ever needed the fires of purgatory, it was this last-minute convert.

Yet there is no hint here of penalty or punishment. One thing is luminously clear: death for him was an entrance into the unveiled presence of the Lord. We don't know very much about heaven. In fact, we know precious little. But we know this, and this is enough. Tell a believer that one day he will be with Christ forever, and that is all the heaven he needs.

Did you ever think of how those two thieves, one on Jesus' right and one on his left, stand for all of us? Luke likes to picture things that way. Remember Simon the Pharisee and the weeping woman? Remember the tax collector and the Pharisee in the temple? Remember the prodigal son and the elder brother? All of us are represented in each scene and will finally stand in one camp or the other.

In a sense, it is not a case of the sinners over against the righteous. There are sinners on both sides. No, the truth is that we are either repentant sinners or self-righteous ones, either penitents or prigs. Our misdeeds will not condemn us at the last unless we have scorned the mercy that could blot them out. Our hope is simply and only this, to be among the sinners whom Jesus saves.

1. What does the word salvation mean to you? Do you see it primarily as negative or positive (salvation "from" or salvation "for")? Do you think of it as past? Present? Future?
2. From this passage, what would you consider to be the essential steps to salvation?
3. Is "feeling guilty" the same as knowing that you have sinned against God? Explain.
4. Is the experience of the penitent thief a good warrant for postponing repentance until the final days of one's life? Explain your answer.
5. What other New Testament passages indicate that believers are brought at death into the Lord's presence? How is this related to the hope of the resurrection?
6. How would you respond to this remark: "That thief on the cross certainly wasn't as deserving of salvation as a person who has served Christ for many years!"

24

CHRIST'S EASTER MESSAGE

Background Scripture—Luke 24:13-49

> *Then he said to them, "These are my words which I spoke to you, while I was still with you, that everything written about me in the law of Moses and the prophets and the psalms must be fulfilled." Then he opened their minds to understand the scriptures, and said to them, "Thus it is written, that the Christ should suffer and on the third day rise from the dead, and that repentance and forgiveness of sins should be preached in his name to all nations, beginning from Jerusalem. You are witnesses of these things. And behold, I send the promise of my Father upon you; but stay in the city, until you are clothed with power from on high" (Luke 24:44-49).*

Just what did Jesus say to his disciples on Easter? The four Gospels present several scenes in which he appeared to his followers, together with snatches of conversation and brief summaries of what he taught. But there must have been more—much more.

Have you ever wondered, for example, how the disciples, who seemed so confused about everything before the crucifixion, could proclaim the Christian message with such clarity and conviction after Pentecost? Their power and boldness came from the gift of the Spirit. But whence came the content of their Gospel?

Here again, Luke gives us information that no

other Gospel provides. He stresses that the risen
Lord spoke to his disciples at length about the Old
Testament Scriptures. The first mention of this is in
the account of Jesus' encounter with the disciples on
the Emmaus road.

Two travelers have been discussing the recent happenings in Jerusalem. The conversation reveals that
their understanding of our Lord's ministry is limited.
He is to them "a prophet mighty in deed and word
before God and all the people" (v. 19). They had
hoped that he was the one to redeem Israel, but they
don't know exactly what to make of the angelic message that he is alive. Jesus chides them for this. In his
eyes, they are "foolish men, and slow of heart to believe all that the prophets have spoken" (v. 25).

They should have understood, but since they don't,
our Lord proceeds to teach them. "Beginning with
Moses and all the prophets he interpreted to them in
all the Scriptures the things concerning himself" (v.
27). They saw Jesus as "mighty in deed and word";
he assures them that he is the Christ who should
suffer these things and enter into his glory" (v. 26).
They saw him as a prophet, but he presents himself
as the one to whom Moses and all the prophets bear
witness.

Later that evening, the risen Lord appeared to the
disciples gathered in Jerusalem. After he had made
himself known to them, he took up the same theme:
"These are my words which I spoke to you while I
was still with you, that everything written about me
in the Law of Moses and the prophets and the Psalms
must be fulfilled." "Then," we read further, "he
opened their minds to understand the Scriptures"
(vv. 44-45).

Notice what is happening here. There is a kind of twofold ministry of Christ to his disciples. He is taking them through a course in the Old Testament, showing them how in each major section—the Law, the Prophets, and the Writings—the ancient Scriptures bear witness to him. It is Christ himself, in other words, who directs his church to a Christ-centered interpretation of the Old Testament. This doesn't mean, of course, that its every verse must have an explicitly evangelical reference, but it does mean that the Old Testament record of God's saving purpose is fully and rightly understood only in the light of Jesus Christ.

But Jesus not only pointed out these Scripture portions to his followers; he also "opened their minds" to understand. They needed not only a master teacher to explain the truth, but also a divine illumination to grasp it. Apparently, then, no man can rightly interpret the Old Testament until his eyes have been opened to see Christ as its central theme.

If we only knew which Old Testament passages our Lord discussed and exactly what he said about them! This we are not told, although the subsequent teaching of the early church suggests a number of key passages to which he probably referred. Luke, however, does give us something vastly significant. This closing chapter presents our Lord's summary of the Old Testament message as it relates to his own ministry: "Thus it is written that the Christ should suffer and on the third day rise from the dead, and that repentance and forgiveness of sins should be preached in his name to all nations, beginning from Jerusalem" (vv. 46-47).

Here, then, are three great events toward which

the Scriptures point, three motifs running through them all: Christ must die, he must be raised the third day, and repentance and forgiveness of sins must be preached in his name among all nations.

This is the heart of the Bible's message. It is God's purpose that people throughout the world should find forgiveness and life through the crucified and risen Jesus. For this the world was made. For this Israel was called and fashioned as God's instrument. For this the church was born. These things, according to Jesus, must come to pass.

This "must," this idea of necessity is strongly stressed: "Was it not necessary that the Christ should suffer?" (v. 26). "Everything written about me . . . must be fulfilled" (v. 44). There is the pressure of a divine compelling about all three of these events. Isaiah's prophecy had stressed this long ago about Messiah's suffering: "The Lord has laid on him the iniquity of us all. . . . It was the will of the Lord to bruise him. He has put him to grief" (Isa. 53:6, 10).

Jesus picks up this theme in his own teaching: "The Son of Man must suffer many things and be rejected by the elders and chief priests and scribes and be killed" (9:22). And so he sets his face like a flint to go toward Jerusalem. He prays: "If it is possible, let this cup pass." But it is not possible. He must drink the cup. He must endure the baptism. The Son of Man "must be lifted up."

The same momentum of destiny leads to the resurrection. Jesus says: "The Son of man must be raised on the third day." Peter on Pentecost preaches that it was "not possible" for Jesus to be held by death (Acts 2:24). Paul rings the changes on how essential, how imperative the resurrection is—how everything depends on it. If Christ is not raised, preaching is a falsehood, faith an illusion, redemption a failure, and hope a mockery (I Cor. 15:12-19). All the Scriptures bear witness to this tremendous event. Christ must rise.

But what about that third necessity—the preaching of the Gospel to all nations? This, too, must come to pass. Jesus says, "I have other sheep, that are not of this fold; I must bring them also" (John 10:16). But there is something different about this third event —something that sets it apart from the first two. Christ died and arose again—that is past, but the bringing of the message to all the world is not yet fully accomplished.

The second difference is even more significant, The first two are completely God's doing—we contributed nothing to his atoning death or his triumphant resurrection. But this third necessity, this third element in his purpose, is one into which we as believers are drawn. We don't know why, but he has entrusted this task to us. The salvation of the world depends upon it, yet God has placed it in our hands.

1. What is the evidence for a substantial teaching ministry of Christ following his resurrection?
2. According to Luke 24, what is needed for a full understanding of the Old Testament?
3. Does this mean that Old Testament believers did not really understand their Scriptures? Explain.
4. What does the passage suggest about the importance of prayer preceding our study of the Bible?
5. How should the thought of God's sovereign purpose affect our outlook on the work of the church? How does it make you feel?

25

A JOYOUS FAREWELL

Background Scripture—Luke 24:50-53; Acts 1:9-11

> *Then he led them out as far as Bethany, and lifting up his hands he blessed them. While he blessed them, he parted from them. And they returned to Jerusalem with great joy, and were continually in the temple blessing God (Luke 24:50-53).*

Imagine it—they were seeing his face for the last time here on earth, yet they turned homeward rejoicing. And he was the best friend they ever had! How could they be happy at such a parting?

Luke is the only Gospel writer who tells us about Christ's ascension. John has Jesus predicting it (John 20:17), but only Luke describes the event itself. For him it has pivotal significance. It is the final happening in his Gospel and the first in its sequel, the Book of Acts. And it is Luke who records the strange fact that after the disciples had seen their Master taken up from them, they "returned to Jerusalem with great joy and were continually in the temple blessing God" (24:52, 53).

Luke's Gospel, then, ends on the same note with which it began, with God's people worshiping in the temple. We can understand the note of gladness in the opening scene, when the birth of John the Baptist is celebrated. But what about this postascension joy and praise with which Luke concludes?

First of all, the ascension made the disciples glad because they saw in it a kind of enthronement of Jesus. They had known about the triumph of his resurrection. They were assured "by many proofs" (Acts 1:3) that he was alive after his suffering. Now when they saw him being taken up from earth, they understood it as an exaltation, a raising of Jesus to heavenly dominion.

At this point, the faith of Christians is often misunderstood and caricatured. The Russian cosmonaut, Titov, felt that his orbital flight had made Christianity ridiculous. At a news conference in Seattle he said, with amused contempt, "Some people say there is a God out there in space. But in my travels around the earth all day long I looked around and didn't see him. I saw no God or angels." Others hold that the velocity required to put a satellite into orbit, the Van Allen radiation belt, and the cold of interplanetary space prove that the ascension is impossible. Christians are laughed at as those who still believe, even in the Space Age, that heaven is up and hell is down.

The early Christians, however, made no attempt to locate spatially where it was that Christ had gone. They knew from his resurrection appearances that the risen Lord though recognizable, had entered into a new sphere of existence in which he was free from ordinary physical limitations. His ascension was an event of another order entirely from, say, a space flight. When we confess that Christ has ascended, we affirm that he reigns in the very presence of God. And wherever he is, there is heaven.

But could even that thought bring rejoicing to the disciples? Could a faith in his heavenly dominion nullify the grief and emptiness of separation? The ascension meant quite evidently that Christ was gone from this planet—gone for good. There would be no more resurrection appearances, no more surprises of a well-loved face and voice. From now on, He would be in heaven and they on earth. Could they be joyful about that?

The joy came because of Jesus' promise. John records it like this: "I will not leave you desolate. I will come to you" (John 14:18).

Christ ascended—here is something to rejoice about. We have a Savior who has conquered sin and death and hell and who reigns upon the throne of the universe. Though we do not see him now, we are united with him in a fellowship that nothing can break. One day he shall return as he ascended—this time in glory and power to reign forever. The brightest joy is still ahead!

1. *What significance has the ascension of Jesus had for your faith up until now?*
2. *Why do you feel that the ascension receives so little emphasis in the preaching and teaching of many churches?*
3. *Do Christians believe that heaven is a "place"? Explain your answer.*
4. *What do we mean by the confession that Jesus is now "at God's right hand"?*
5. *How can believers experience the presence of Christ more fully now than the disciples could during Jesus' earthly ministry?*
6. *How has the prospect of Christ's return affected your outlook on life?*